ENTWINED GENRES: COLLECTION OF 30 BLOGS

Based on True Stories of Modern Life

Swapnil Roy
'SOULTINKER'

Chennai • Bangalore

CLEVER FOX PUBLISHING
Chennai, India

Published by CLEVER FOX PUBLISHING 2024
Copyright © Swapnil Roy 'SOULTINKER' 2024

All Rights Reserved.
ISBN: 978-93-67071-82-3

This book has been published with all reasonable efforts taken to make the material error-free after the consent of the author. No part of this book shall be used, reproduced in any manner whatsoever without written permission from the author, except in the case of brief quotations embodied in critical articles and reviews.

The Author of this book is solely responsible and liable for its content including but not limited to the views, representations, descriptions, statements, information, opinions and references ["Content"]. The Content of this book shall not constitute or be construed or deemed to reflect the opinion or expression of the Publisher or Editor. Neither the Publisher nor Editor endorse or approve the Content of this book or guarantee the reliability, accuracy or completeness of the Content published herein and do not make any representations or warranties of any kind, express or implied, including but not limited to the implied warranties of merchantability, fitness for a particular purpose. The Publisher and Editor shall not be liable whatsoever for any errors, omissions, whether such errors or omissions result from negligence, accident, or any other cause or claims for loss or damages of any kind, including without limitation, indirect or consequential loss or damage arising out of use, inability to use, or about the reliability, accuracy or sufficiency of the information contained in this book.

To My Parents,

For Raising Me To Believe That Anything Is Possible!

To All The Characters,

Those In Real-Life Who Inspired Me To Write Their Stories!

To All The Readers,

Who Would Benefit In Someway After Reading This Book!

Park the Emotions that Spark,

It's the End of Night so Dark.

You are not a Slave of Monarch,

Make a Life like Gold in Hallmark!

~ Soultinker'

CONTENTS

Preface ....*xi*

PART 1: About Life..1

Chapter 1. Songs of My Soul..3
Chapter 2. Love-Laden Diary Entry of 2003 7
Chapter 3. Understanding Men – Mission
Impossible for the Women!.......................11
Chapter 4. Blessing: Married to My Childhood
Friend..19
Chapter 5. Creating My Space: A Place Called
Home!..23
Chapter 6. Quench the Soul: Write 31
Chapter 7. An Extra Marital Affair 35
Chapter 8. Panchayati Chowki 39
Chapter 9. Life Lessons: Renovate Yourself................45

PART 2: Parenting & Old Age.........................53

Chapter 10. Insights: the Day I Saw My Baby 55
Chapter 11. Dealing with Baby Blues: Experience Based 59
Chapter 12. The Sands of Time: Learning Patience With Kids! 67
Chapter 13. It Takes Two to Tango! 73
Chapter 14. My Tiny Spooky Storyteller Girl 77
Chapter 15. My Man, As A Dad… 81
Chapter 16. Warming Up the Winter of Life 85

PART 3: Social Issues......................................91

Chapter 17. Let Me Crib it All Tonight! 93
Chapter 18. Story of Abundance: Breaking the Shackles 97
Chapter 19. Story of Scarcity - Dahej, A Tradition 103
Chapter 20. Reveal: Don't Instigate Me 109
Chapter 21. Conceal - the Real-Life Nightmare! 113
Chapter 22. The Addict 117
Chapter 23. Curse: Married to A Monster in Disguise 125
Chapter 24. Reach Out, Before the Death on Diagonal Lane 131

PART 4: Life & Death 137

Chapter 25. Style Up: Your Sealed Lips! 139
Chapter 26. Ignite the Durga in You 143
Chapter 27. Weakness - the Last Diary Entry 147
Chapter 28. Is Suicide On Your Mind? 153
Chapter 29. Grief- the Murder Story 159
Chapter 30. Mystical- the Beautiful Ink Black
Heart 167

Epilogue 173
Acknowledgement 175
About The Author 177
Books By the Author 179

PREFACE

*E*ntwined Genres is a collection of 30 blogs that I wrote past 3 years. It has modern short stories based on real-life situations and events faced by various people around me. I am so happy to present this book to you as it comprises of heartfelt real-life experience-based collection of blogs and write-ups.

An interesting part of this write-up is that you can find CONTRASTING Genres to read, find insight and food for thought from every story. Wishing you an entertaining read and insightful journey as you explore each write-up!

PART 1

ABOUT LIFE

CHAPTER 1

SONGS OF MY SOUL

It's a usual new day, when I am done sending my two kids (a seven-year-old son and a four-year-old daughter) to school, freshened up and straightaway headed to the 'Pooja Ghar' for the routine prayer.

$\mathcal{W}$ell, it's a simple sentence, which if detailed, contains a whole lot of story in every 'phrase'. Like, "sending the two kids to school" sounds to me like "SENDING THE KIDS TO SCHOOL" and that any mother can relate to, isn't it? And how may I leave this opportunity to pour my woes and not tell you about getting up early each day, preparing the Tiffin's, breakfast for kids, water bottles, shoes polished, school dress, time-tables, pencils sharpened, and ID cards in place and many such very small things, which if not done, maybe a reason for a diary notice from school.

Then comes the part of cuddling the kids and asking them to wake up, then coaxing, then reminder one and reminder two and countless and then threats come into the picture. So they wake up, and then the final part is helping them with the smallest things from putting the toothpaste on the brush to tying the shoelaces, one by one, they both kiss me goodbye as they leave for school. The daily rush-hush part is over for the day... Sigh of relief... Peace prevails!!!

So, I drink a glass full of water and take a deep breath, and the real good morning begins now. I grab the newspaper, get a hot cup of tea and later freshen up and head to my 'Pooja Ghar'. So, begins the real story now. (oops, after I probably already used half of my blog space...)Don't laugh ... Not yet... Let the child in me wake up now!!!

As I clear the previous day's flowers, cleaning up my Pooja Ghar, I also start chanting my prayers learnt since childhood, the ones already remembered even by the tongue....Then suddenly, after a while, my ears hear something... I realize myself singing the tune of some Bollywood song!!! OMG!!! How could I? Mind speaks to heart and I find myself wondering, does it happen with others too? Does it happen to you too? The Mind is at peace, and subconsciously, singing its tunes... N after I consciously stop uttering those songs and get back to Mantras... Again, it's turned into some other song in a while... A bigger OMG! And then it's like effortless next gesture of seeking forgiveness from the heart, directly to my lords! Oh God, I will try not to do this again and I will focus on the rituals to be done and meditate for a while closing my eyes...

After a few times, it happened on various days, and now and then, I found myself thinking about it. I captured a moment when my kids do their prayers in such a natural way before they leave home for school. They tell God all the good and bad intentions they have for a fun-filled day, and ask for any help if needed to save from mom's and mam's scolding! Also, they tell God to take care of all while the kids attend school... N finally waved goodbye to Gods. N sending off the flying kisses... yeah, to Gods!!!

I also remembered the ways to meditate or pray, as told and shown and practiced by many family elders. Some methods preached by religious profiles on media or in person at worship places also flashed across my mind. Everyone has a different way... Some are God-Fearing, some are God-Loving, and some even don't believe in an entity called God and contest other opinions of some divine power... And all are correct in their own perspective.

So, it's surely a personal choice how you want to believe you were created, and this world and flora and fauna and human beings arrived on this Earth. Surely a prayer made with pure intentions or even a thought sown into mind with goodness is foreseen will fill your heart with positivity and when your soul is happy, full of hope, so pure somewhat like kids, your day will be good, your life will be fulfilling!!! You may chant prayers or sing the songs of your heart... I am sure you will be blessed with the joy of soul!

Stay Blessed... Let the child in you, within you thrive with joy & love!

CHAPTER 2

LOVE-LADEN DIARY ENTRY OF 2003

I took out my long-lost diary, in which I used to write, about 20 years ago. It was wonderful to revisit it and find this entry, close to my heart, that I will be sharing with you all today. It was a time when "our love story" was blooming.

*I*t's related to my present husband, who was "a friend" at that time and had proposed to me a while ago, earlier in that week! I hope you enjoy reading it, thanks!

....

Diary Entry Dated: 03rd April'2003

Dear Diary,

When I was in Kathmandu, I had some long chat sessions with "him." He was in Patna. For 3 days, we had chats on Messenger for an hour or so in the afternoon. As usual, we were fighting and teasing each other, remembering our school days and cherishing all those golden moments. The last day I was chatting with him, somehow, I realized how much I miss him and also that his situation is somewhat similar to mine. I don't know why, but I feel like he also likes me a lot.

This is not new, as we have always had something, some bond, that connects us. We call it friendship, but we are best friends. I never realized when or why I had started liking "him" so much. It's nearly 10 years since we first met and 8 years since we became friends. We had always been close, but there had never been any kind of commitment like love. I never thought it was possible between us. C'mon, I mean, I still don't believe it! We always teased each other, fought, and shared our moments of laughter and pain, but c'mon, no romantic evenings or love talks ever! Actually, I was always looking for someone who would love me, and I would also love him, but I never realized it could be "him"! We loved each other just like friends do, not in that romantic or eternal sort of way. But this time, when we met, it was different.

While chatting with him on the net, somehow I knew that this time if we met, we would have something to think about. I felt his inclination and mine too. To tell you the truth, Diary, I have always "liked" him. From the first day we met in school, we had a certain bond between us. At first, I assumed it was attraction, or perhaps infatuation! Then it appeared to be a similarity of preferences and attitudes. With the added spice of fights and misunderstandings, we thought it was friendship. But... has it matured enough to know if it is love? It had always been there. But we were searching for it elsewhere in the entire world.

I can't remember a single day that has passed when I have not thought of "him." I couldn't ever forget him, even if I tried for those long years when we were not together after school. I tried to suppress my feelings for "him" for so many years, but it's truly said "love finds its own ways. I intentionally tried to keep any serious heart-related matters away from "him," but this time God wanted us to tackle this long-overdue talk. "He" had always asked me, proposed to me, and told me his feelings, but all in a casual way, never seeming to mean it. I thought it was all because we were such close friends. When my closest friends, S&S, told me that "you both are made for each other," I laughed at them and said, "HE? NEVER!" I never knew that I meant, "YOU? FOREVER!"

I don't know how I managed "not to say a straight yes" when you proposed to me on the fateful evening of March 26th, 2003. You so sincerely proposed to me again and again. I saw commitment in your eyes. I have not yet officially accepted your proposal, but I am sure you know it. I'm just making myself sure of my feelings for you, and I will tell you a straight "yes" or "no." I want to keep our emotions crystal clear! That's all for today diary... see you very soon again, with the climax of my love story!

CHAPTER 3

UNDERSTANDING MEN – MISSION IMPOSSIBLE FOR THE WOMEN!

My Man and I have a superb mutual understanding, as in – he doesn't at all understand me, and even I don't at all understand him !
— **Soultinker**

*A*nd I am sure that most women reading this would agree with the same about their man. So dear ladies, what is it that we women don't understand about men? The moment we women connect, we surely find some common ground, against men. But even living under the same roof, sharing the same room and bed, and spending a full lifetime together, also leaves us quite clueless about how this particular breed of male thinks and responds, especially about 'relationships'! Here is my story of a dating couple Meghna and Sumit, who showcase the typical scenario of how men and women do not 'just' have different wavelengths, but also they belong to different worlds of some distant galaxy!

It was a beautiful beginning. Meghna and Sumit met at a common friend's party and had a blast of a time together. There was a mutual liking, and they exchanged numbers. Soon after texting and chatting for a few days, Sumit asked Meghna out to a movie. She accepts and they have a good time together. After a few days, he asked her out for dinner, and again they find solace in each other's company. They began to see each other regularly, to the extent that they did not see or date anybody else for that matter. It was all good and made them both feel good in each other's company.

Then one evening when Sumit was driving back home to drop Meghna, a thought just popped up to Meghna. She says, " Do you realize that we have been seeing each other for almost a year now?" And there was a pin-drop silence! And since Meghna spoke the last words, this silence was too deafening for her to bear… Soon she started thinking to herself, "OMG! What the hell did I just say? He got so silent…may be feeling uneasy that I am taking our 'friendship' too seriously. Maybe he will think that I am pushing him into some kind of relationship obligation or something like that. How I wish, I hadn't said that!"

And on the other side, Sumit thinks, "Gosh! One YEAR???" <Full Stop >

Meghna thinks further, "But well, why bother, even I am not sure if I want to be in a relationship with him either. I mean, is our a-romantic relationship of that serious kind? I mean, heading to marriage? And kids? And family drama and all that stuff? A lifetime 'with Sumit'? Is he 'the' guy? Do I know him thoroughly? Am I even ready for that kind of commitment?"

And Sumit thinks too. "One YEAR means we met at the New Year Party, last January… and soon after that I gave my car to the dealer for servicing, and later we started going out… So must be like the second week of January… that means it's been such a huge overdue that I got the car serviced, not even the oil change, gosh… I should get it lined up soon. Even the engine sound seems like a roar…"

Meghna is now wary of the silence. Thinking loud in her mind, "He looks upset and reserved. Maybe I touched the wrong chord. He may need more time to figure out if we can enter a relationship or not. Maybe he just wants to hang out with me and not think further? Maybe he is not sure about me… isn't that why he has not yet proposed to me in all these months? Or I am not sure if he is scared of being rejected?"

Sumit has no clue about the happenings in the silence! He is occupied with his serious business… about the car repair! "This time I will get the estimate for the dents and painting too… all those small scratches here and there. And will have to send it on a weekend holiday or some festive time, so that there is no commutation issue. The Bumper was greatly dislocated last time with that stifle with that biker… that needs to be replaced, maybe, if not repaired. Will get the clutch and brakes checked too, there is this screeching sound sometimes nowadays. Will have to check the warranty dates and all tonight."

Meghna thinks, "Looks like he's angry. Not uttering a word! I feel so guilty for making him so wary of us. Don't know what to do now. First and foremost I should stop thinking like a schoolgirl wandering in a fairytale world… and it's not the era that a knight will come riding on a white horse and fulfil that ageless fantasies of a woman being desired by a man…! What a stupid thing I said… ruined the evening for him…"

Sumit thinks, " Just after dropping Meghna off, will go home and first look for the car papers, insurance and ownerbook… and tomorrow will line up for the suitable date for sending the car to the repair and servicing centre."

"Sumit", Meghna says aloud.

"Yeah", says Sumit.

"I am so sorry that I am such a fool… I mean, I know it's not the ancient time, and there is no Knight and there's no white horse.", Meghna says sobbing.

Sumit, in utter confusion, "There's no horse?"

"Do you think I am a fool? Or a nagging one pressurizing you?" says Meghna.

"NO!", Sumit says, truly glad to know the correct answer to this twister kind of question. Already nervous as what more question pops up, and did he miss out on something in her life about the white horse?...

" I think I need some more time to sort this thing in my mind… We need time." Says an emotionally vulnerable Meghna.

Sumit searches for a safe response… and takes another few seconds… finally says, "Yes!"

Meghna feels so soaked with haywire emotions. She holds his hand, and says, " I am sure you don't take it otherwise and are comfortable thinking like this?"

"Comfortable thinking about what?", Sumit asks in doubt and desperation.

"…about taking time?", Meghna says full of emotions in her eyes.

"Oh, Yes!", Sumit still feeling nervous and giving out short answers was extremely unprepared for the next question. The Thank you, and goodbyes, and he drops her home and leaves for his dwelling place.

Meghna felt restless with the swell of emotions, thousands of questions troubling her delicate mind and love-lorn heart, she lay in bed and cried her heart out… She is sleepless till dawn, checking their chats and messages over the past months. She took out the gifts he had given her and the notes on them, that she kept safe in her drawer and in her memories. She re-lived their first meeting and the fun outings and comfort that they shared. She then fell asleep.

Sumit reached his room, sank into his bean bag with a packet of chips and a cold drink, tuned the TV to the sports channel…and was fully engrossed in watching the cricket match highlights of two foreign countries! There came a tiny pop-up in his mind, saying that something unusual was happening back there in the car… and Meghna was occupied with something, but he soon realised that he shouldn't overthink about daily things!

Meghna called up her best friend forever "Saanvi" the next day and gave every painstaking detail of what each said and felt and did last evening. The pros and cons continued to be discussed for the weeks after that without reaching definite conclusions and not also being bored of it. Saanvi would ask her for the updates for any further talks with 'him' regarding that evening. Meanwhile, Sumit after a few weeks met a common friend of his and Meghna in the cricket club, and paused to ask 'Rohit' casually, "Did Meghna ever try horse riding in her childhood or what?"

So, what we are dealing with in this story of a man and a woman is not about perspectives of understanding or different wavelengths of a male and female brain. We are looking at the fact that 'men and women' are aliens that have been put together on Earth! The man's analytical & problem –solving brain is messing around the delicate heart of the female focusing on love, trust & relationships!

Women cannot even imagine that two people who spend so much time together and hang out exclusively with each other, will 'not' be thinking about the depths of their relationship… But dear ladies, please get this straight… your man might be sincere for you, but still needs to be told and reminded now and then that he shares a 'relationship' with you… and that after hundreds of such direct and indirect reminders, one day you might be lucky when his brain registers this information and tells his guests on the 3rd or 4th anniversary be, that he and you have a relationship! His truth!!! Such are our men, and such is our plight of a woman… never tired of trying out deciphering the codes to understand the men.... Categorized into Mission Impossible!

Hail the Men & Women living together, in bliss', on this Earth!!!

CHAPTER 4

BLESSING: MARRIED TO MY CHILDHOOD FRIEND

No two people can be exactly alike. It's unrealistic to expect that they think and act as per others' expectations.

Over the years of staying together, spouses get used to each other to a great extent. They learn to accept each other with their several shortcomings. Given the good times and common interests that they share, if they start adjusting to create a good rapport with their partner, it lays the foundation of a good marriage. In the same context, it can be imagined what it would feel like to marry your childhood friend who has known you in and out for years… It's indeed a Blessing… a Marital Bliss!

In my case, marriage was an additional chapter in the story of our TEN years of 'JUST' friendship and FOUR years of full-fledged love affair. So before tying the knot of marriage, we had already crossed the 'Vanvaas' of FOURTEEN Years of knowing each other thoroughly. We were schoolmates, also classmates but never in the same section. And from the very first day of my admission to school in class 8th, my (now) hubby was aiming for my heart in every way he could. Never mind, this cupid was known for flirting all over and was never taken too seriously by me. But now, as I see our past, the memories of childhood are beautiful indeed, and all thanks to 'him' for making it so colorful and happening. We fought like kids, we kept missing each other but continued 'not to talk' for months, we fought for each other's attention too, and major and minor issues came up now and then. Every six months or so in our affair – there came a phase of 'breaking up'… but regardless, we found solace only with each other and no one else could replace that void!

Sometimes we laughed in between our fights because the other one would know the exact lines and thoughts that would pop up. And EXCEPT the fights which are an intrinsic property of any marriage, we were love-birds of our time! Lost in a fairy-tale kind of love for years… Doing all the lovely things of the Late 90's like writing letters to each other, which became love letters in the after-years, and that land-line missed call era, meeting secretly, surprising each other in festivals and places…

a beautiful and romantic train journey that he took to give me company from hometown to the city where I studied…A lot more that will stay with me as the sweetest phase of my life forever!

Before we declared it to our parents and friends, we were questioned individually like, "What are your plans? When are you two planning to tie the knot?" Neither of us ever had the opportunity to look for alliances meet people and explore the rest of our options, Alas! Having said all the above, it doesn't at all mean that love marriages don't have compatibility or adjusting-together issues. It does have everything just like an arranged marriage, but yes, it makes it easier to understand each other and offer a helping hand to cross the disturbances. Also, you are already done with a lot of fighting and making up, so you know what works for you and what doesn't.

Jokes apart, it's best if you both are friends at heart, comfortable sharing anything and everything with each other. If this element of 'being friends' is still intact in a marriage, it might be the strongest bond of life. In many years, TRUST has found a place as easy as breathing. It's beautiful to see more such childhood love stories maturing into blissful marriages… This also gives way to new social equations as caste-creed, religion, ethnicity, and dowry all take a backseat and just love prevails.

May God bless us with the beauty and joy of staying in friendship and love for a lifetime!

CHAPTER 5

CREATING MY SPACE: A PLACE CALLED HOME!

10th May 2014 is one of the most cherished days of my life. On this day, I made a major decision and shifted from all my temporary dwelling places existing in the whole big world to A Place Called Home... So glad, that it's my home! It's difficult to tell you what kind of nomadic life I felt like before this step that changed my whole life for 'good'. Here is my true story, which feels like a daring venture... even after all these years.

$\mathcal{B}$oth my 'Mayeka' and 'Sasural' are in one city and not very far off from each other. After the wedding, I shifted to my sasural, an old but big and well-maintained duplex house, where my room was on the upper floor. It was a beautiful room, specially developed with false ceilings, floor carpeting and new furnishings for making me comfortable living there after marriage.

Thanks to my in-laws and parents for being so thoughtful. Ours was a love-marriage, meaning that hubby 'was' more like a friend than a husband to me. He was then, a second officer in Merchant Navy. In the initial 2-3 years, I was happy staying there... as for more than half of the year he would be sailing, and I would join him onboard for several months at a time. We visited many countries and it was like an extended honeymoon.

Meanwhile, my in-laws found their innate love for the city of Kolkata in Bengal, mostly as they are Bengalis by culture... and my FIL got fully involved in building a new house, a bungalow, home to my MIL, in Kolkata. Soon after that, they mostly spent most of the months in Kolkata, where an additional joy to them was staying together with my SIL, whose husband is a banker and was posted in Kolkata. My ordeal began then, as every time they moved to Kolkata, I was given a day's notice to shift to my parent's house, as the duplex was unsafe to stay alone in a city (my hubby was sailing). And whenever my hubby returned from the ship, OR my in-laws took a trip to maintain the ancestral house, I was expected to be back there.

It meant that after every 2-3 months, there was a complete shift required for me! It was not just the place that changed, but the complete set-up, timetable, and living conditions. Also can't even explain the ordeal of cleaning up the closed house, full of dust and spiders every time I made a move back. My personal belongings were scattered between the two places, Mayeka and Sasural. While the third dwelling place, joining the ship, was not so regular afterwards due to other obligations in the picture, like my 'dadi saas' stayed with me, when my in-laws stayed in Kolkata to build their house. I was getting tired, more so mentally.

And then I became pregnant. I was advised by the doctor to be mostly on rest for the initial few months and to avoid steep stairs. So from the duplex with my room on the upper floor, and in-laws not staying there for long months, there was no one to take care of me, I had to be completely shifted to my Mayeka. Though both my parents, mom and dad were working, still we lived together in a cozy and comfortable flat, where it was easier to stay safe and sorted of daily things, better than that in Sasural. I spent the full tenure of pregnancy, childbirth and the initial year of my first baby, mostly in my Mayeka.

I had also started to work, as I cleared the exam of a government organization. But the moving out every few months when my husband came back from sailing continued. Later, he stayed sometimes with me and my baby at my place(Mayeka), else would have to stay alone in his ancestral house for maintenance sake... and also due to social obligations like - my in-laws didn't much like the idea of 'him' staying at 'his sasural' for a long time. Things started getting sour between us. I would hate to stay away from him even when he is back from sailing and is home only for a few months. He had to cater to his parent's expectations to stay with them either in the ancestral house or visiting them in Kolkata. Also, my parents were suffering to see me torn between the struggles of managing this nomadic life... and also because they got so habitual of living with the toddler grandson that it hurt both sides, for them to be apart after every few months.

Tearful goodbyes happened every time, and it broke my heart to see my son crying to stay with his nanu-nani, while I had to shift to sasural. And my hubby was also going through the same mental pressure, that got him to stay forever angry... sometimes with me, sometimes even with the child, as he saw him getting cut off from his ancestral house and his parents for the matter of 'attachment'. But then, attachments can't be forced. It comes naturally, especially by spending time together... And that my toddler did with his nanu-nani, undoubtedly. Years went like that... and issues started cropping up between me and my husband. We loved each other, but faced a situation, not acceptable to both of us... living apart in the same city! Our arguments and discussions never ended. We were suffering.

My mental agony was to the level that I told him that even if it was on rent, I wanted to move to 'my own place' where I could follow a normal life and routine with my toddler, now grown-up to a kid ready for schooling. I couldn't change his school every 3-4 months. Things needed to be sorted. But my hubby had the baggage of, can't move out leaving my parents in the ancestral house. To which I reacted as they hardly lived there, just a couple of months in a year or so. Rest they lived in the new bungalow that they built in Kolkata and even my SIL had shifted there to stay together with her family. Nothing seemed to move, except me and my baby.

In the timeline, it was already about 7 years of marriage, and my kid was now 3 years old, nomadic like me! In one of those fits of anger, my husband went sailing without even talking to me, and we had stopped communicating except when needed for almost 'six' months. I was losing it, was so full of apathy. Then, once he returned from sailing, as a chief officer, he approached me, and we headed for a patch-up... He agreed to look for a 'flat' of our own to shift in. We booked one, but it was still under construction.

Time elapsed. I was pregnant with my second child. And I was restless about my nomadic living arrangement. I told him to move to a rented flat till our purchased one is completed. Though he was against the idea of being on rent out, he agreed to go for buying out another ready-to-shift-in flat instead. With God's grace, we found one and bought it with great difficulty in financial arrangements. I had to listen to some touches of sarcasm in this course, that I was responsible for anything that happened to my hubby due to such financial burden he is bearing for 'my' sake. Well, I don't know if I was having a blast of a time either in all those years of turmoil! Nevertheless, that's the usual way the jibes are meant to be, towards the 'game planner' foxy clever insensitive overambitious wife! And again, my hubby had inhibitions about how to shift, when to shift, what his parents would say about it, what the society would think of it... and what not... and with all these rippling thoughts he better joined his ship again, off for another 5-6 months. I was aghast.

I had made up my mind. I was ready to be portrayed as a selfish woman. I was rather hoping to be a decisive mother. I was 3 months pregnant and also had a 3-year-old kid. I found an auspicious date from Google and my known astrologer, and ANNOUNCED my decision to the whole world - my hubby on the ship, my in-laws in ancestral home, my parents at Mayeka! That I am shifting to 'MY HOME' on the 10th of May,2014, come-may-whatever!!! Mostly, all of them had the first concern of how will I manage kids, pregnancy, household and shifting, a full-time job, all alone... but I had just one agenda on my mind, it's now or never! Reasons will never end. Later they will say your baby is about to be born, it's too small to take care of alone, why leave in-laws alone and move, next- it's okay and safer to stay with parents in Mayeka now that your husband is adjusting to visiting there frequently.... NO, NO, NOOOO... I had to end this pattern.

I wanted a place I called HOME!!! And I shifted all alone. My parents helped me with setting up everything - from new pieces of furniture to kitchen essentials. My hubby always caters to the finance of the matter. My in-laws didn't like it, but didn't object to my decision... as I never asked but only declared my final decision. I hope they understand now, that I really had to do it!!! Else we would have damaged emotions and relationships to an irreparable level. A servant, who helped me take care of my kid and household was a great support to me in those days, I always thank him from the bottom of my heart.

All said and done, in the final month of my pregnancy, my husband came 'home' - our home, when he didn't have to think whether to open his luggage in his wife's Mayeka, or ancestral home or should first go and meet his old parents mostly found in Kolkata. He was happy too. I had settled in my home. Planned and made it comfortable for him, for us, in every way possible and suitable. I had also called up my in-laws and invited them to stay with us whenever they felt like shifting back here, in 'our' home... where I was even comfortable and safe living all alone, only with kids.

This was one of the best decisions I took in life. Now, even after 16 years of Marriage, and 9-10 years of living here, I am still happy about my decision. It made my family happy too, our marital discords ended, our kids shared a great bond with all four grandparents and finally, five years ago, my in-laws quite old now and struck permanently with medical issues have gladly shifted back from Kolkata to live with us. My Mayeka is closer to my new flat, and I can look after my aged parents too. My kids often go and stay there with Nana-nani, and all this arrangement works beautifully for now. This is a story, real-story... heartfelt and close to my being... it gave direction to my otherwise, nomadic life.

Writing this blog today, from this place that's my favorite in the whole world - ***it's a place I call Home!!!***

CHAPTER 6
QUENCH THE SOUL: WRITE

The only major difference between a 'Writer' and an 'Author' is 'a published book' !!!

$\mathcal{A}$ **general notion about writers:** Before I started writing blogs, I did have a notion about writers. Those who write professionally are writers. Those who have a flair for writing, (even though they don't write professionally) may also be called writers. Writers are people who are very literary, intellectuals, who have a passion for writing, enjoy their work, mostly are serious kind, lead a lonely life for their love of writing and so on. A few elderly people added their wisdom, saying that writers are so lost in their thoughts that they exist in the most basic/simple settings and unorganized spaces with papers & books scattered all over. They hardly care about anything else except reading and writing and thinking in between! I am afraid but, I am nowhere near that! I wonder if ever I can be a renowned writer without these traits fulfilled.

Amateur Writers- At present, I am not sure what the future holds for me as a writer, but for sure I love writing. It's like a vent out, where I can pour my heart out articulately. I may not speak a lot or may not be heard by many, but when I write, people 'have to' read, even if they agree or not... or scroll away! They may not change what I wrote. That makes me feel so powerful. So, I would like to tell you about the life of an amateur writer like me! Since 'NEWNESS' is attached to amateurs, I find it such a passion to write nowadays. I feel like writing about anything and everything. Ideas appear from here & there.

After a few good write-ups, even the readers start suggesting what to write. You are never short of topics. Well, in the long run, or maybe sometimes when you are not in a mood, there might be a 'blank' or writer's block. But it's just temporary! Despite all this, the best part of writing is that it *'quenches the soul'*. If it stops doing so, you may stop enjoying to write... and such work doesn't give you satisfaction.

Life of a writer- It may not be generalized because life is unique for everyone. You may be a full-fledged writer or just doing it part-time as a hobby. According to it, life would be different. What's common in most writers is that the mind is at work all the time!!! You may be thinking, creating in your mind, imagining, planning a plot for your write-up, looking for clues & ideas from something you come across and so on and on. Amidst all the happenings around you and in the whole world, your mind is busy weaving stories. It makes you more sensitive towards people too. You tend to see, hear and learn their experience to a level that you understand what it might have been to feel it or how would it feel like to be in their place.

> *The life of a writer helps you to feel the emotions of your character in a story. It makes you accept the world as it is.*

Hidden Secrets of a Writer- To the best of my understanding, every writer has a 'secret hunch', that works only for her. It might be the clue she picks up for the topic chosen to write, the format taken, the titles or headline, the timing of publication, also the people or medium to reach out to, and personal network, all of this takes shape in some time. But it is all hidden and it's surely a secret that every writer has, knowingly or unknowingly. The writer's hunch about all of the above is the most important characteristic that keeps the work going in the chosen direction. Those whose equations work right, make it to success, fame and money. Others might have to slog. A little luck and a 'good strategy' definitely make the journey of the writer easier. This so-called 'good strategy' becomes the hidden secret of a writer.

Hope you find yours and I find mine - good strategy soon... and for that some love and mutual support would be wonderful to make us feel lucky and move on with zeal... *Wrapping my words now, as too many secrets must not be revealed!*

CHAPTER 7
AN EXTRA MARITAL AFFAIR

Blooper at first - Never did I ever, have an extramarital affair !!!

As I speak of this, let me tell you where this idea appears from. I had a beautiful love story, which was my first and the only love affair I had, but that turned into the bond of marriage. Sounds perfect? Have you ever heard of any famous love story that ended in marriage? Consider Heer-Ranjha, Romeo-Juliet, Shirin-Farhad or be it like in movies like Jack-Rose in Titanic, Salem-Anarkali, Bajirao-Mastaani and the list goes on and on... These had a tragic ending and became immortal!!! The love stories that end in marriage, become household stories, not a love story any more! It loses the charm and adventure of an affair.

Well, I am not being thankless for a good life, but you definitely have to pay a price for everything you choose in life... If you grab one thing, the other option is lost... as is the case of love stories! A beautiful memorable love story, or a mundane, similar to next-door neighbor kind of marriage saga! In my case, my sweetheart became my husband, and you know what a typical Indian husband is like- MIL's trophy that she can't stop boasting of and will be a disaster if he puts his plate in the sink... He perfectly fits the criteria of all else, except - anything and everything around household work and kids! So, I told him that I crave a love story... something tangy and spicy in life, like if I had an affair! My dear husband smiled at me, and said, that it isn't possible to be just an affair but a Extramarital Affair now, because we are already married! Bingo... so I told him that since you have a trail of affairs before you committed to me, and I had none, you have to be accommodating if I get into an extramarital affair, at least once in this lifetime.

Our conversation went on for days and days tickling each other about the possibilities of my such plan... that too with my husband taken into confidence and, additionally, he is absolutely not allowed the same privilege because he already had it before our affair in the past. He agreed, only with his overconfidence that you won't find anyone other than me matching your fairytale standards and no one would volunteer to keep up with your "*nakhras*" and "*kharchas*"... how dare he!!! Once he shared it with a few of our very close couple friends, their wives voted for me and joined in the campaign. To the disappointment of my husband, their husbands volunteered and gave their availability for any such possibility. Men will be men! To brush them off, I simply put my criteria, and that conditions apply that he has to be a stranger in the first place!

And c'mon man, seriously... in my fairytale kind of world, affairs just trigger in a moment... it's about that gushy-mushy eye contact when you know in your heart that something clicked between us! It's not at all intentional and doesn't require to be tried for, it just happens like a miracle! And myself in my 40's such eternal kind of tickling love stories don't surface up quite often. So, the possibility is open... and the search is on!

The man I will have an extramarital affair should be a stranger to me. And then my list of terms and conditions include that, he should match my wits and have a great sense of humor, have a husky & manly voice, should be classy in treating me with ultimate love and care, should be genuinely interested in me, should put efforts to win me, should treat women equal but show his manliness in respecting and standing for them in need, should love me for the way I am... and so on and on... n then he must be capable enough to keep me in my luxuries and comfort zone! Basically a Mills & Boons character, I guess!!! And then my childhood friend, my love, who is also my hubby now, chirped... that "HE" is the only one I am looking for again, what a pun...

I will not give up this time... let me dream tangy and wait till I tell you if I turn this 'Never had I ever - have an extramarital affair' into "Story of my extramarital affair"... Wish me luck, ladies!

CHAPTER 8

PANCHAYATI CHOWKI

Nostalgia prevails as I think about the favorite piece of furniture owned by every household in India... it may come with a different name and build, but in some form or other, it surely exists in a cosy corner of every home.

*I*t's the 'Panchayati Chowki' on which rests the sole responsibility of connecting to each and every member of the extended family fondly called 'khandaan'. For anyone who doesn't know the Hindi words, 'Panchayat' means a village council owning responsibility for self-governance of the village matters; 'Chowki' is a sturdy wooden seat or bed; 'Khandaan' here means a clan on lineage. So, our 'Panchayati Chowki' is a sturdy piece of furniture in a comfy corner of our home where we lie and adjust and share the 'Dohar' and gossip about every spicy event on the globe with multiple rounds of tea... 'garma-garam chai ki chuski'! And mind you, gossip here is actually a 'panchayat' that includes discussing pros, cons, alternatives, emotions, choices, possible solutions to others' problems and whatnot... The best part is that one story emerges from another and again and this 'panchayat' continues session after session. No one is spared, be it immediate family or relatives, friends or acquaintances or even the celebrity or complete strangers whose news might be read by someone in the newspaper. Here is my story of nostalgia about the 'Panchayati Chowki of my khandaan'!

Since childhood, when we- the cousins huddled together during the summer vacations, we saw the adults calling up each other and making space in the room on and around the 'Chowki' to participate in the 'panchayat'. I remember my eldest of cousins Rishi bhaiya calling upon me, "Chalo mausi, Panchayti Chowki lagai jaye aaj... maine chai ke liye bola hai..." And all the adults will come giggling. Either 'Banaras' or 'Munger' was the city, the hub of our summer vacation holidays and it's the story of the 1980's and 1990's... Looks like ages but the memories are still fresh. Kids would be busy eating juicy mangoes and discussing whether 'Malda Aam' is tastier or is it 'Dushehri Aam'.

Then suddenly they had an idea of copying the 'Panchayati Chowki' idea of adults into 'Bachho ki Chowki' on which they will play the 'Pass the story' game for hours... laughing out loud at the funny takes of each notorious brother and teasing sister. And the ongoings of 'Panchayat' goes like this:

Badi Mausi, "Arey wo Manu ki nanad ka pata hai? Unki beti ne bhag ke shadi kar li... wahin Kanpur me. Waise to sab maan jaate per Hindu-Muslim ki shadi me aaj ke zamane me bhi sochna padta hai... Rahan-sahan baat-vyavhar taur-tareeke, sab alag hota hai na"

Nani, "Achha! Fir hua kya, ab to bahut mahine ho gaye honge?"

Lucknow wali mausi, "Hona kya tha, dono Mia-biwi alag rahte hain, dono ke pariwar ne naate-rishte tod liye hain. Bechaare bache, rah rahe hain akele. Ladka achha job me hai, engineer hai. Ladki bhi parhi likhi hai, kuch kar hi legi."

Rishi Bhaiya, "Aaplog updated nahi ho. Abhi ek mahine pahle ladke ka accident ho gaya bike se. Bechara critical tha. Plus wife do mahine pregnant thi. Bahut pareshani me the wo log. Aage ka pata nahi.'

Banaras wale mausa ji, "Arey pata karke batana zara. Ab jo ho Gaya so ho Gaya. Karli bachho ne shadi apni marzi se, per ab to gussa chhor ke pariwar ko support karna chahiye. Samjhayenge hum Manu ko... apni nanad ko bhi samjhaye. Bachho ko aise me chhor dena thik hai kya?"

Nani,"Bilkul sahi, ab to bado ko sambhalna chahiye. Ladki to apni hai na. Mai bhi samjhaungi."

Lucknow wali mausi, "Mera to milna hota rahta hai, mai bhi yahan se wapas ja kar milne jaungi. Sab thik karke batati hu. Waise Rishi tumhe kaise pata chala?"

Rishi Bhaiya,"Wo ladka jis company me kaam karta hai, wahan mera dost bhi hai 'Maithili' wahi bataya tha. Inter-religion marriage ke chakkar me mausi ne mere se bhi pata karwaya tha us ladke ka background. Wo Shantanu ko janti hain na."

Nani, "Arey kafi din huye, Shantanu ka kya haal hai? Suna foreign gaya tha office ke taraf se?"

Badi Mausi, "Hahaha.. arey Rishi se mat pucho, uska pakka dost hai... aur isko bataye bina foreign se shaadi karke aa gaya! Russian ladki hai. Itni sundar, kya bataun... aur abhi banarasi bolna seekh rahi hai!"

Rishi bhaiya, badi mausi se, "kya mummy, aap bhi na. Mujhe bataya tha Shantanu ne. Per achanak shadi kar li to India aake hi to batayega na!"

Lucknow wali mausi, "To abhi ek din ghar bulao na un log ko khaane pe. Milna bhi ho jayega. Nayi bahu se mil bhi lenge. Aaj kal to foreigner se byaah karna 'trend' hai... apna Bollywood hi dekh lo. Affair karte hain yahan, shaadi foreigner se karke ke aa jaate hain." *giggling*

Nani," haan chalo thik hai, aaj sham baat karte hain... bulaate hai Shantanu aur uski dulhan ko ghar pe, per abhi sab thodi neend le lo. Khana khake thoda sona chahiye dopahar me! Raat ko fir laga lena Panchayati Chowki. Tab mai bataungi ki meri shaadi ke baad kaise saas ke taane sunne parte the... sipah salar bulati thi mujhe, fir bhi nibhaya hamne, tum log ko kya pata..."

One story after another. It went on and on. It's been several years. Many of them are no more - my Nani, Rishi Bhaiya, Banaras wale Mausa ji... Rest are dealing with old age, still connected. We kids have grown up and entered mid-life. But such memories of warmth and relationships still hover at times. The gadgets and different lifestyles have faded during those summer vacations. Earlier we used to be twelve to seventeen cousins meeting during summer vacations. Nowadays, in all, there are hardly five to seven cousins in all, thanks to smaller and nuclear families. Plus they are not so connected, like the kids before the millennium.

Things have changed. Some are good, some not so good. We must accept that life changes every moment, and over the years one feels like a generation gap somewhere. Let's not judge right and wrong, but we surely can share these small stories to keep some warmth flowing down the clan, to the kids and new generation, so that they don't grow cold to the people around. I hope they enjoy sitting together on the 'Panchayati Chowki' too and relish the memories in their old age. The worth of things changes with time. But warmth and good memories always find a place in our otherwise cold hearts.

Middle-Age transforms and filters you through the generations... I am in this phase, pondering over the speedy changes past few decades. And really missing out on the 'Panchayati Chowki' of the past and its participants... their real-life stories still afresh in my mind, endearing voices in my heart.

With remembrance to the lost souls!

CHAPTER 9

LIFE LESSONS: RENOVATE YOURSELF

Once upon a time, there lived "I"... Who didn't look like me, didn't sound like me, didn't even feel like me, and didn't even behave like me... The way I do today!

Sometimes I am unable to recognize myself, the way I perceive myself and the way I find people think of me! Is that how we have changed over the years? Does it happen with many of us or maybe most of us?

Amongst all the big and small things that life is supposed to be, one thing agreeable by each one of us is that life is ever-changing! Even the one who has monotony as a constant companion, can't escape the change of time ticking in the clock and date on the calendar, also the greying hairs and the change of scenario due to the movement of other people in the vicinity. And just as opposed to it, there are people (like me) who are either criticized or appreciated, for changing things a lot... I mean, a hell lot, you know, and quite often! So, be it a change in the arrangement of bed and sofa, color of walls and curtains, texture of furniture and floor, complete wardrobe change in the new season, bringing in the new timetable, new activities and hobbies, trial recipes (including disasters), and the list is as never-ending just like the course of life. One word that fits all the changes I initiate is "Renovating"...and I am sure most of us would find it to be a rather warm word to encompass all our "change urges" to a modest level.

We indulged in renovating our home past two months. And all this while, however hard we tried to keep things in control and as per plan, still it had been a messed up household, hard work, too tiring schedule, and sometimes finding day-to-day things was like a treasure hunt game. You may relate to this situation, still, I will mention the dust storm inside the home, the decibels of irritating noise, the smell of paints and chemicals, the absence of workers, overflowing (out) cash and a lot of headaches. This former sentence was only to pour out my woes and be at peace to some extent. But the only idea that it would be over in a short while, and lead to a brightened up, comfy, warm dwelling space for all of us in the family, kept me going. It also leads to mental peace and a more organized daily life.

An important aspect of home renovation has been "retrospection" now and then. Even the simple choices and decisions we make, like the color chosen for a wall, or print chosen for a curtain, or a painting placed somewhere, make us doubt and reconfirm phase-wise, that, it's not bad, it's going to be okay, should I take advice, no... its good and new and bright, let's go for it! Plus you get opinions and advice from almost everyone around you, including kids and laborers and neighbors, and without asking for it. Another learning was that once you start the process of renovating, new ideas keep popping up, and you get indulged in doing a little more than planned. Plus it's an opportunity to discard or renew the various clutters and corners that we usually ignore to touch otherwise. The team of experts from various fields that you meet is another eye-opening experience and makes you learn about the various intricacies of many professions and skills. It's absolute learning, a crash course.

Such projects of renovation, when completed successfully, do give you utter satisfaction and joy of creating and achieving. It uses all your skills and talents which otherwise keep getting tarnished as we may not ever need to use it. Renovation needs multitasking in varied areas. Be it planning, implementing, people management, meeting time deadlines, financial management, negotiation skills, documenting, calculating, prioritizing, decision making, taking risks and whatnot. So, I thought to take this concept to another level and see how can we renovate ourselves... Yes, renovate yourself!

Sometimes when we look around us, a sinking feeling comes up... The walls look dull and old, the things look dusty, the work seems mundane, and even the people around look tired and irritated over small things. In such circumstances, if your focus goes to all the worldly things that can be renewed, repaired, or replaced to brighten up your life, you head towards home renovation. When it's over, and one fine day you again have a sinking feeling, amidst the newly set beautiful home, you know something else needs to be worked upon. When all things look normal to consciousness, peace of mind is missing. You wonder what's wrong, and get to some of the following things happening to you:

1. You don't want to be angry, but can't just help shouting over small things. Your inside tells you not to act in a certain way, nonetheless you still behave improperly. You are angry with the whole world, and the whole world around you is also mad at you. Sadly, you don't even know the reason.
2. Your near ones start drifting away and keep a safe distance from you. They tell you to check your BP and thyroid for any imbalances, and over a heated discussion, some may tell you to visit a psychiatrist for counselling or help.

3. You may have lots to share and say to your friend, colleague or spouse, but you choose not to... so as to avoid any conflict and discussion. Before you even begin to speak, you already know the answers you will be getting, as you know them too well.

And lastly,

4. You type questions on search engines, like, why I get so angry, why people seem irritated with me, why people don't like me, or why I am unable to do things right...

So many things you know about yourself when you just check the search engine history...

Because, that's the best friend for sharing whatever you want, in today's world. It's not judgmental, its answers are honest, it is at the tip of your finger and will never pop up again on its own, and it has strange solutions to all our queries. If nothing else seems relevant, it may at least change your focus to a new game, new question, or a shopping website. So all is good with this new-age friend of ours.

On a serious note, when all the aforementioned things happen, I would safely say, it's time to splash some cold water on your face and sit back, close your eyes and think of ways to renovate yourself!!!

Renovation when alleged to a living being might not mean to restore to a previous or better condition, but it surely means to bring some newness and freshness in your life and spirit... It will be a different solution for each individual. But the guideline remains the same, as,

a. you need to declutter emotions and mundane tasks(similar to giving away useless things to the needy and then throwing out remaining garbage in the bin during home renovation),
b. prioritize things in your present life (the plan of action for taking up renovation, like making the necessary ventilation),
c. change your routine and focus, pick up a new attitude to suit your mood swings, (like we manage time, staff, resources during home renovation),
d. try consciously to overcome the shortcomings that you find true for yourself (like taking professional help for specific work or welcoming suggestions for improvement during home renovation), and
e. choose your behavior to deal with others, specifically, your close ones, allowing dedicated time for them free from hustle-bustle (like we retrospect our own choices and decisions after laborers are gone while renovating home).

All this will require effort, loads of it, and time, more than expected, and patience... that will keep coming and going as you further your aim to renovate yourself. I am sure, we can do this, once when we are willing to, once we try. And why would anyone want to stay angry every day? Why would we like to keep ourselves stressed and irritated? Why should we lose one precious day of life, cut off from loved ones... It's not worth anything!

So, for once, let the words pour out or let the silence fill in, choose to hold your tears or let them flow like a river, pick a new hobby or take out your old crafts to complete, go for a new hair-do or a brightened-up jazzy look, or stay unnoticed - low profile if you like it, do what makes you feel new and what renovates your spirit. It is one life. A beautiful one.

A happy one preferably. So, **Renovate yourself!!!**

PART 2
PARENTING & OLD AGE

CHAPTER 10

INSIGHTS: THE DAY I SAW MY BABY

Being a woman WE have a privilege over the other gender, that can't be denied, come may whatever... and that is nature's gift to feel 'life' grow inside you! Isn't the thought of it overwhelming?

*I*t was one of the most beautiful moments of my life that I shared with my husband standing beside me, holding my hand… teary-eyed, grinning face... we were the happiest on earth! It was the first time we saw our baby on the ultrasound screen. What a miracle of nature, to be full of life, and then get a chance to be reborn when you become a mother... as if you get a new life. It's not just a baby which is born... It also transforms a woman into a mother... the same moment, a mother is born! It begins much earlier than the day your baby is born in this world. It's when you get aware, that first instinct of knowing that you are pregnant, and then you are not the same person anymore, as you have evolved.

Motherhood magically touches EVERY woman. It makes you wonder and awe at your hidden talents and superpowers. However, it also brings fears and insecurities that you never knew existed for you. Motherhood is so divine, that you may only feel... and those can never be able to fully be expressed in words... To be a mother is a miraculous experience. Motherhood makes you connect to a soul, a tiny being. This new one is created inside you and nurtured within your body. It is cared for and protected to be able to survive in the world. Being a mother takes you to another level of Spirituality...It makes you let your heart walk outside your bodily being. Still, you go on mothering your best creation for the rest of your life!

You secretly hope to see your baby to be away from any worries and stay happy in life. All her life, this hope and wish never dies in a mother's heart, whatever her age be. Mother's love begins with the seed implanted and can't end until death. It indeed is the purest form of love visible to human eyes... All the thoughts about the sleepless nights, mischief, multitasking, sibling fights, messy homes, overload of work, professional hiccups, time management going for a toss, and much more into purview... Still, you already know, that you won't ever give up on motherhood for any comfort on this Earth. This is what 'being a mother' is all about!

You are so much in love with your baby that nothing else in the world exists for you at that very moment. Let all the mother and baby souls on Earth be blessed with such pure bliss of love!!! *Thank you Mom for simply everything... And thanks a ton to my kids, who made me understand my mom, finally, by their presence and without even uttering a word!*

CHAPTER 11

DEALING WITH BABY BLUES: EXPERIENCE BASED

"I remember my face when I looked at the mirror one fine day after cajoling my baby to sleep.... The haggard-looking eyes, a swollen face deprived of sleep and a shapeless body!... And the pain and the feeling of loneliness... that the whole world just left me out to this endless job of catering to this baby...and I don't even know how to do it properly..." I cried in my mind... later said the same to my hubby... and cried my heart out!

Being a mother for the first time is a great milestone that is both pleasurable and challenging at the same time. After all, taking care of yourself after going through the birth procedure, whether it's normal or caesarean – in both cases, can be quite hard. Additionally, you are now responsible for tending to the needs of another tiny human being, especially one who is dependent on you. The fact that it's your baby, a part of you, created by you and nurtured inside your body, is the only inspiration that should help you survive every difficulty that will come your way.

I am a mother of two kids. The first pregnancy was surely a learning phase for me. And the next one too was a crash course with the latest updates! However, I was blessed to be guided by my mother, my MIL and also a supporting and caring husband. Still, I remember, during my first childbirth experience, how I cried one night as I thought that the baby wouldn't ever feed on me... later in a day or so, it did! I remember how I got angry with my husband for being unconcerned and sleeping peacefully, while I was up all night... he said nothing but got up and took the baby from me and cajoled it to sleep. Yes, there are not many baby blues, as I read a lot of pregnancy books and talked about it with friends too to get a fair idea. Also, my family has been supportive, especially my husband... and you feel lucky when your spouse takes care of you during the pregnancy, it at least relieves you of one big stress. But all stories are not the same. I did come up with many known friends and family, where pregnancy was too difficult and tiring, especially for the mother.

It is good to prepare yourself mentally, as quickly as possible. You are stepping into a new status... that of a mother to this baby. Trust me, you are not alone in this journey… and most of the new mothers face one or more of the challenges that I have tried to put here for you to relate to and find a little solace.

1. Postpartum blues are a very common and usual phenomenon after childbirth, but often an overlooked complication.

A lot of mothers might have mood swings, crying spells, insomnia, and anxiety… and if you are one of them, don't at all panic as it is part and parcel of this journey. It's not easy to deal with, but it fades in some time. Try to distract yourself from what you're feeling, instead, it's better to engage yourself in taking care of your baby. If it doesn't go away, you should consult a doctor, who may help you soothe her/his experience with many of his/her childbirth cases. Being a first-time mother is not a cakewalk. The first step is usually the hardest. Through the passage of time, some experience, and the help and advice of others, you'll get the hang of how it is to be a mother. And once you do, you'll understand how fulfilling it is.

2. Breastfeeding is not always easy for every new mother!

The best case would be that soon after the birth, the baby is put with the mother to feed, and it can do it easily. But many times the baby would not latch or would not be able to suck milk. It may cry inconsolably, wrenching the heart of the mother. Hold yourself, woman... that's quite common, and it's okay if you have to feed it from outside sources for a few days. Just don't stop trying every time the baby gets hungry, the sooner it latches, the better for both of you. Once it starts, it might get easier day by day.

To be comfortable with it, some mothers and babies may take weeks of practice and patience with each other, but it mostly works. You should ask for help from another mother who has experience in breastfeeding, but never compare experiences. Don't give up too quickly, and take your time to get easy and habituated to the necessary timing and positioning.

3. It might be a period of disturbance or stress in a marital relationship with a spouse.

Trust me, my dear, this is one of the most common problems first-time mothers face. Childbirth and childbearing may put a spousal relationship under strain. It is difficult for anyone to take care of the baby 24/7 and for a new mother, it might be too much to handle. There is physical pain due to the procedure of childbirth, breastfeeding now and then, sleeplessness, and stress if you can do it properly or not. With all this, women may easily feel that their husbands either do not understand how difficult it is or are not doing their part.

Men, on the other hand, may be pressured to provide more for their family, or just like new mothers, they are not sure of how to do their role and what to do. If you and your partner are going through the same tensions, then talk about what you feel about the entire situation, especially if you think he's not helping.

'Communication' is key during these hard times, and asking for sharing the workload by holding the baby for some time cajoling it to sleep, or changing its nappy would give some consolation to the mother, and make it look worthwhile to both as parents!

4. The mother's pre-baby figure might be distorted for a while, causing you concern and making you feel low.

Don't you envy celebrity moms for being able to get rid of the extra weight they gained during pregnancy, as they put every other work taken care of by professionals and spend a huge amount and effort for same? You are no way even near that, right? Don't let that trouble you now because it's completely normal to retain a few pounds after giving birth. It's also normal to miss your pre-pregnancy body, but you have a lifetime to get back to your fitness regime and take care of yourself to get back in shape. Now, it's time to cater to the baby and enjoy your motherhood thoroughly.

5. Other worries like career, work, leaves, being a working or non-working woman, health issues of a self and newborn baby, taking care of the elder child, mood swings of new father, missing out on previous life, outings, friends etc.

My dear Lady… Forget these blues for now and till the time it doesn't become the priority, more important than your baby. All this is unimportant NOW, at this moment. And for sure can be taken care of in a later stage. Knowing that it's normal and happens with almost all of us women, just chill yourself. Keep a positive frame of mind, and you will sort this all out later. You are too good to manage your life, and you will get even better after dealing with this newborn. So, just let it be the way it is, and focus on the most important thing you have, this bliss called 'your baby'!!!

Being a first-time mother can be extremely hard, especially if you are not prepared. Read some books on maternity. Subscribe to some magazines for motherhood. Talk to friends who have been through it. Ask them to be honest about the challenges, and get handy tips. Talk about the good times as well, as this tiny baby of yours will soon grow up, and then you will miss this initial phase.

Community plays an important role, so it's a good idea to surround yourself with other first-time mothers who are going through the same thing as you. If nothing else helps, at least you will feel comfortable to know that it's not just you and this phase… It's about every mother who gives birth to a new soul. If the troubles are yours, so are the smiles and the very firsts of your baby. Try to learn and handle things to the best of your capacity. Soon you may end up feeling blessed and lucky, rather than a victim.

All the very best… to the best mother of all – and that's surely you… You are faring well, doing a good job, and soon you will yourself feel to be the best mother to your baby… *Just give it time and have a little patience!*

Happy Motherhood!!!

CHAPTER 12

THE SANDS OF TIME: LEARNING PATIENCE WITH KIDS!

The sands of time are just slipping off in every moment... and it's been years after years, and the learnings never come to an end. Now this blog is a learning revisited, as a mother of two sweet naughty kids.

"Unless I shout, no one will respond in this house. Am I simply inaudible in my normal voice? Can't anybody hear me when I say something for the first time? Don't make me lose my patience again... I am already short of it !!!"

Is it just me? Or is it the story of many more moms on this planet? Well, this has been my everyday story past many months... and I so very much get pissed off hearing my loud voice... because I am not cut that way.

I had a very different opinion of myself as a mom! I believed in not raising my volume and had faith in talking sense to be heard and understood by people. I also thought it to be a behavioral privilege to be able to talk logically and convey my thoughts clearly to the other person. But it's a parallel life as a mother. Here, the giggling of the kids never ends how politely I ask them to sleep. The dancing doesn't end even after the night lamps are switched off and they are put to bed. The study time never ticks on the clock unless I shout my heart out.

The playtime never ends and increases every 5 Minutes then 10 Minutes then 20 Minutes of its tenure until and unless I put my red face and angry eyes specifically on the two demons who have all the abilities to turn me into a crazy woman. And once I was out of my patience and raised my voice already, these notorious devils with their innocent faces looked engaged in what I had 'politely requested' of them one hour ago. And look at the facial expressions... it makes me feel like a culprit... the one who is a habitual crazy woman... ruining our fun & games, always trying to put us under discipline - knowing how we never intend to give in to such boring good habits, and now that it's too much, 'sorry' comes to an easy rescue she falls into! Yes, a few emotional lines-

'Mom, won't you wish us a good night, as we are about to sleep?'. 'Sorry Mom, please help me do this homework,

I can't submit it tomorrow if you don't help me… please Mom.' 'Just 5 mins Mom, I am going to take a bath, don't shout.' … "Oh no Mom, are we getting late for school… please help me get ready and reach school on time, please Mom don't be angry now."…

And my anger has a flip side, as a mom. They always know how to keep their temper and volume down when their father is around, to save them from his more dangerous wrath. Yes, that makes me boil with uneasiness inside, but just limit myself with some threats of spilling out the beans and letting them imagine the consequences… Oh, this role of a mom!!! I don't know whether I do it right or wrong, but hearing similar stories of other moms, of the endless dramas of dealing with the monster munchkins, I feel that I am not alone in this world pulling my hair out.

And then finally I read a prompt, a quote… 'Not to hold the sand too tight, as it flows out quickly!' After a fresh incident of shouting out to my kids to sleep in time, I felt like taking a deep breath and applying this quote to my scenario too… yes, I chose to loosen myself a bit. Let them do what they feel like. I switched off the lights and went to bed. Left them still playing in the drawing room. My son is 11 years old and my daughter is 8 years old now. Too friendly with each other when they have common interests, else just the worst enemies ever spilling out the beans about each other to me! So, it was another 15-20 Minutes and I heard them whispering in surprise. And they slipped into bed beside me. They were not sure if I was angry at them, or upset, or both... they very carefully put their small hands on me. Then, on getting no response, hugged me closely... said sorry, and then goodnight... "We are sleeping now, mom"! I felt happy, it worked.

Again, the next day I told them to complete all the schoolwork and that it was my first and last reminder for the day...If a remark comes, your father will be informed, as I am too tired to deal with both of you...! And I left the scene... Not that magic happened, but yes, after delaying it for some time the elder one was seen on the study table doing his stuff, and his sister followed him in the deed. A small magic that brought some relief to my heart!

Thought of continuing this, of saying once and leaving the spot completely for them to decide and take action. Maybe it will take some time, but even teaching about responsibilities, is not a worthy lesson for the kids. I am on it, presently. And definitely, even I am not too old to learn again that we sometimes need to change our approach and let go of things not serving us anymore. Shouting was against my nature and made me feel sick for the whole time if I did it... Also, there was a fear in my heart that my kids would drift away if I got too harsh on them... but letting go felt like a peaceful way of dealing with the same issue. I consoled myself that they are born with their destiny, and I can only try to support them with my little understanding of life. To be strict with my timetable is fine, I will not try to control them with a raised volume. I have been peaceful since then.

Something reiterated in my mind, once I talked with a close friend in a relationship crisis... and we together agreed that relationships - of all kinds - are like sand held in our hands. Held loosely, with an open hand, the sand remains where it is. The moment you close your palm and squeeze tightly to hold on, the sand trickles through your fingers. You may hold onto a little of it, but most will be spilt. Better, we hold relationships with respect and freedom for the other person, it is likely to remain intact. Even if it doesn't, you will learn to let it go and not blame yourself for the loss. But trying to control or hold it too possessively, even when it's about the small kids, it may ruin the sweetness and natural bond and make it feel like a burden.

Attachment can't be forced. It has to be nurtured slowly, with time. And a mother needs a lot of patience to deal with kids. There is no other magical way out of this role. Even the most impatient woman of all becomes a statue of patience in the role of a mother... I can see myself as an example! Sometimes I also want to add to my thoughts that it's good to wish and hope and work towards strengthening your relationships earnestly, but it's best not to expect the same in return when it involves another person in the picture... *practicing to let go...* as a mother, again in this phase of life!!!

CHAPTER 13

IT TAKES TWO TO TANGO!

"Bhabhi, I just love the way you look cool even when the kids scatter all the toys in the room", said my SIL as I looked back at her.

I was not even interested in glancing at the kids out there, who were enjoying- that would mean, shouting-jumping-quarrelling-dancing and throwing toys while playing together. It made no sense, as they would not stop! So, most of the time, I choose to speak to them only when I fear that they may hurt themselves by playing in a particular manner. Rest is all good. I am okay with clearing up the mess created when many guest kids are involved and doing it in one go. It's like wrapping up all the drama. But till then, I enjoy 'peace of mind' and allow them to have loads of fun together. The guests don't know my plight, since both my kids are in the same school, I am used to their 'Dangal' and the makeover from morning to dismissal time. It's like they were not studying in a classroom, but were rather wrestling in mud.

My 'Be Careful' attitude comes into play, especially when my 'younger one' Miku, is in a rowdy mood. She is 8 years old now. She is immaculate in her being except that she reacts to her Bhaiya's teasing! My 11-year-old boy is aptly talented in teasing anyone to a dearth level. He can bring out the mad mom spirit inside me! And when these two quarrel, I don't want to be the referee... but who else will be? On the verge of them being running after each other, pushing or beating, shouting or crying... I have to become the referee!

"Mahi, For Godsake, STOP teasing your sis? After all, you are his elder brother! And...

Miku, come whatever, I don't want to see you scratch Mahi Bhaiya again... and this is my last warning to you!!!"

This is my everyday story! And trust me both kids involved in whatever messy situation or turbulence, are equally involved in it and share the responsibility... and I make sure that both are punished equally too!

These notorious two are always a team when it's about elders vs kids and would enjoy their so-called kids' time by singing, dancing, wrestling, yes, wrestling and so on & on. And it was just yesterday that my son came with a bump on his head and narrated how he fell from his bed.

Yes, it seemed a simple explanation but not convincing enough for me seeing the size of the bump, no way. So yes, cross-questioning and investigation began. My little daughter was all prepared for my queries to answer to save both of them... but then she is just 8 years old cute one... To my stern look, she would blurt out."

Bhaiya is always teasing me... to mai to marungi na?" While bhaiya is standing behind the curtain and giving words to her sister, to escape my anger... But I am too tired and fed up to be angry anymore. So, it was an episode of bhaiya teasing, little sis losing her temper, then a wrestling session, followed by both of them falling off the bed and returning hurt to mumma!

When it is not an episode between elders' vs kids, they are at the absolute cross with each other... one complaint after another lots of arguments and no valuable discussion! It's like the end of the discussion when Miku will shout in anger, "Mahi Bhaiya MERA bhai hai, isko sirf mai marungi"- We all burst into laughter. But that's for real. She won't let any other person harm her brother, will protect him, but afterwards will beat and scratch him too... I so call them 'dramebaaz' and that they surely are!

The moral of the story is that both are equally naughty in their fields and leave no stone upturned in annoying me with my referee role... and I am too tired and in the end, the only thing I keep coming up with that makes me subtle is 'Be Careful, don't just hurt yourself and each other, you two ... "*Definitely, it takes two to Tango!!!*

CHAPTER 14

MY TINY SPOOKY STORYTELLER GIRL

Young children from the time they learn to speak, often make up stories and tell long or short tales.

This may be treated as a normal activity for kids because they simply enjoy hearing stories from teachers, parents, grandparents, TV shows, Cartoons etc. and so they also start making up stories for fun. These young kids may sometimes be found to blur the distinction between reality and fantasy, like my younger one – My daughter Miku. She is a super duper talkative enthusiastic 7-year-old being whose stories never come to an end. It goes on and on and on. We sometimes have to tell her to practice "Keeping Quiet" for 5 Minutes or 10 Minutes and confirm that by watching the time on the clock… The toughest activity for her! It makes her restless like anything, and she will start moving around, jumping, controlling her giggles, putting a finger on her lips dancing here and there and whatnot! But this jolly tiny being dares to spook us in real… and that's from the time when she was just a toddler.

Here is her contribution to making one of the world's shortest (probably), yet best spooky stories…

She was about one and a half years old talkative baby. And my son was around 5 years old then. My husband was far away, sailing on his ship, while I stayed alone in my flat with these two kids of mine. It was late at night and I was putting them to sleep. I had a red light fixed on the false ceiling that I used as a dim light before the kids slept. Miku had a habit of drinking a bottle of milk in my lap as she drowsed to sleep. It was summer, and the fan and air-conditioner were full on. Her eyes were wide open, and she was playing with her fingers and drinking milk from the bottle. Suddenly she stopped, looked over my face at the ceiling somewhere, removed the bottle from her mouth, and spoke… "Mumma, ye pankhe ke upar kaun baitha hai?" Trust me, I didn't dare to look up. And I lost words for a moment. And had a little fear in my heart even after I put her to bed and thought lifting my gaze to the ceiling!

Now she is grown up a little, still wants to hear this story from me again and again and laugh like hell. Now, she has an imaginary friend called 'Chintu' who has been her constant companion for years. She will talk to him, race with him, and even blame him for doing things that I would have scolded her for… so it's her escape too! She will even tell me that he goes to school with her though 'mam' never gave him a roll number. And sometimes she finds him to be the only audience to hear her never-ending stories of animals, princesses & avengers, and cartoon characters, even her school friends and teachers. When she does not have many friends to play with, she is constantly with 'Chintu' and playing with him happily. She will ask for extra chips and Maggi for him too. I don't discourage her, but do tell her, "Chintu ko bhi khilana, khud mat kha jana!!!" She keeps herself engaged creatively speaking on behalf of her characters, spinning stories in which she is the cutest and the best one, awed and appreciated by everyone, and her elder brother 'Mahi bhaiya' is at the losing end in every live or imaginary battle they have with toys in hand. To me, she will say, "Mumma, aapke baal kabhi upar hoke seedhe khade ho jayen, to samajh jaana abhi aap pe Bijli girne wali hai! Aur agar koi storm aate aate ruk jaye, to matlab, wo speed me aake aapko apne ander kheench lega, bach ke rahna!" I don't know why I am the victim of such imagination.

Thankfully, her spooky stories are disappearing day by day, and she is more engrossed with stories portraying her as a celebrity or queen or the bravest of all, and we love to hear her narration of everyday stories from her school. She is blessed with the qualities to engage us as an audience and even strangers become a fan of her storytelling in no time. Storytelling provides children with a window to new worlds… the world of Imagination! It allows them to be creative and to learn new ideas. Even without realizing it, they are learning valuable life lessons through making and telling engaging and exciting stories - that have a problem and also a solution… Isn't it amazing? I wish we adults too could have a happy time living in our own imaginary world, creating our own characters and stories and living happily forever after… making it the best closing line ever.

The world of storytellers is full of possibilities. It has hope, love and inspiration, that such a life is possible amidst all ups and downs of life.

> *Kudos to Storytelling… and our tiny natural-born storytellers !!!*

CHAPTER 15

MY MAN, AS A DAD...

We have been married for 16 years now and have two kids aged 12 yrs old son and an 8 years old daughter. My husband is a Captain of the Ship, while I am a stay-at-home mom.

*L*ike always, when my husband was about to go sailing on a ship for another tenure of a few months or so, I simply followed the routine. I told my kids that I would drop them off at Nani's place for a couple of days so that Papa could do the packing and wrap up his work before he left for the ship. Very casually I told about this plan to my husband, and immediately saw the topic 'From My Husband to a Dad' reflect on his face!!! And so I chose to write this piece, after a long time, what pours out straight from my heart... My Man, as a dad...

I mean I knew he always wanted to spend more time with me before he left home for sailing, and that he wanted to have time with me away from kids... but in that moment, he looked troubled. He said that he would be leaving in two days, and then won't be able to spend time with kids. "So send them after I leave"... Well, I surely followed but was also amazed to see this new trait, rather a huge transformation in his thoughts and words compared to earlier years. I was thinking, and feeling good about it.

I have seen him care for me and the baby during pregnancy. I have seen him wait at the door of the maternity room to be the 'first' one to hold his baby... and he looked so emotionally charged as he took my firstborn son in his arms cautiously, lovingly, carefully. I fall in love with him all over again in his new role. Even when my second one was born, our daughter, 'he' was there... but took the elder one in his arms first to show his newborn sister to him and didn't let him feel left out. I loved that gesture.

Now as they grew that tiny new girl who is 8 years old, is the 'Apple' of his eye! He adores her for her style and makeup, for her being so organized and mature even at a small age, for her clarity of choices she makes, for independence and caring nature... and even a lot of "nature", and many traits that he says is just like her mother. Also, the naughtiness of our elder one, son, now 12 years old, brings a twinkle in the eyes of my hubby. Yes, he relates to the boyish things my son does, and he likes a few things out of it... my son is interested in car racing, and mission games and collecting those Avengers and Hot Wheels and stuff like that... I see the joyful expressions it brings to my hubby's face. They did have a few outstation trips and also had some boy's day-out now and then, and it made me anxious at first but when they returned happy, I became the happiest one to see that it went well. There have been times I asked him to deal with kids in a certain way as per situation need, and there also have been stages when I found his anger too heartbreaking for me and my kids, but then with every passing year of life, some tough episodes turned into a learning, that made us all grow strong as a family.

To cut a long story short, I could see his love pouring out for the little creatures who entered our lives during those initial years.... when the baby looked even more tiny in his well-built arms and body. On nights when I got too tired, he sometimes took the baby and tried to put him/her to sleep. He gave me advice on dealing with kids' issues even when he was far away on the ship for his duty. He never interfered in how I dealt with growing up my kids due to the nature of his job that kept him physically unavailable for more than half the year... but still, he was there for me and the kids in every other way, be it mentally, emotionally, financially and always supportive in every way he could... he still is there, especially when I need to hold his hand in small and big life's decisions.

Like every other family, we do have issues sometimes, difficult situations differences in opinions at times, and arguments that might have been better avoided... But in all of this, we do find him like a protective circle around all of us, his immediate family.

To me, his transformation from being a batchmate, to my friend... then to a lover and a fiancée, finally to my husband and then a father of our two kids... I love him in all his roles! I love the memories of how we grew up together in all those past years... and I could see my childhood sweetheart grow up from a romantic playboy to a responsible young man who took my heart away... and then a fun life partner who is also such a caring, loving and amazing father to our kids! He still amazes me in all the charming ways he deals with life, keeping his family as a priority amidst all his life's endeavors and loads of adventures. Thanks for being the MAN of my life, and a responsible but fun parent to our kids!

He still amazes me in all the charming ways he deals with life, keeping his family as a priority amidst all his life's endeavors and loads of adventures.

> *Thanks for being the MAN of my life, and a responsible but fun parent to our kids!*

CHAPTER 16

WARMING UP THE WINTER OF LIFE

Just like the seasons of the year, life seems to operate in seasons. Some parts of life are Spring exhibiting new beginnings, Summer warming up the heart with its usual pleasantness, and Autumn bringing refreshing change along with some nostalgia of goodbyes. And then, as certain as ever, Winter season arrives.

The chilling cold, bitter harsh season that indiscriminately tests the mettle of all of us. It also tells us how strong we are, as it leaves long-lasting lessons! Here is a story of the 'winter of life'... Old age!

When life's winter seasons fall upon you, it may be through the loss of a loved one either by death or separation, the end of a great chapter in your life, or the sudden termination of some routine, some usual everyday thing that you couldn't imagine ending, and we are overcome with grief. How could this happen? How shall I survive? Why did this have to happen to me? Will I ever be able to recover from this? It looks like the end of joy as if life is just over! Winter is harsh, it has a way of testing the resolve of people... but also rewarding those, who show grit and determination, with the hope of spring.

'Baba' as the whole world had been calling him for the past many years after his voluntary retirement was in his 80s, brimming with the confidence of doing all his things on his own. And he had his better half alongside, fondly called 'Amma ji' by everyone, just a couple of years younger than him. Every morning Baba would open the windows of all rooms of their flat for fresh air and go to the east-facing balcony to sit there sun basking. Amma would bring them a flask of tea and two elegant cups, to keep serving and sipping for quite some time while they read and discussed the newspaper and other worldly gossip. With the fall of winter, every year they sulked a little due to the effect of age.

Amma was talking loudly mostly to herself in the kitchen," ...why do you have to be so punctual in sitting on the balcony every morning? As if the sun will go away if you don't appear! Last night you were coughing and sneezing... why can't you stay wrapped in a blanket and sit peacefully in the bedroom for a few days in winter... I just can't understand!"

While Baba was basking in the sun... he paused to wave to someone on the third-floor balcony of the apartment just on the opposite side of the road. Smiles exchanged. Soon he got up and took the bottle of water from the kitchen to water the few plants on the balcony. The same gesture followed on the other balcony, the boy sitting on the wheelchair, watering the few pots in reach. The small kid in the wheelchair drew something in the drawing book he had on his lap and showed it to Baba. With whatsoever he thought was drawn, Baba gestured to the kid showing his hands in appreciation. Soon Amma entered the balcony with the tea tray in her hands, and Baba moved his hand gesturing 'good' towards Amma. She blushed pinker than her fair delicate wrinkled skin. She hid her smile by going back to the kitchen to bring some cookies to have with tea.

Amma and Baba had their flask of tea sitting on the cane chairs and reading and talking about the news and also plans for the day. They would try to connect to their son settled in a foreign land considering a suitable time for his time zone. They would also calm their daughter married far off in a metro city. They will see their grandchildren on the video call and ask about the drama competition and fancy dress in school. Soon after the tea was over and Amma was busy clearing the tray, Baba would gesture to the boy to have his medicines. With this everyday routine on his mind, Baba had the will and courage to show up on the balcony every morning. They both had a bond, an unsaid, unspoken bond of encouraging each other in going through the winter of their lives! Such beautiful people and stories do bring back hope and zeal in life.

On the fifth floor, there met the retired Mrs and Mr Sinha and waved a 'hello' to Baba. They were a comparatively younger couple in their late sixties. Living alone after retirement from a government job, both husband and wife had been enjoying their old age by visiting various places on the globe. All was good until that one day winter fell in their lives, as Mrs Sinha slipped during her morning walk and broke her leg. After a major surgery and knee replacement, she was still practicing to walk with support. Mr Sinha too got busy catering to her health condition and household to the best of his abilities. They trusted their resolve, taking life as it comes and being stronger each day than they ever thought they were.

Just then the call bell rang, and Amma was so pleased to see their neighbour Mr & Mrs Mukherjee had dropped in for the morning coffee as they returned home from the park after their morning walk. Mukherjee had their two sons posted in other cities and a daughter living at some distance so as to visit them sometimes. All four oldies sat under the sun and enjoyed some light moments of laughter and hope over a cup of coffee. When they found themselves in life's winter moments, they thought to endure this, or perhaps even enjoy, this season of life.

You're a lot stronger than you think. Just like winter, life's difficult moments will pass. They only add to our story, but we are alot more than our circumstances. Remember to support each other when need be, invite your friends & family into your life with open arms, and take care of yourself during the winter chill. The sun basking and the warmth of lonely hearts will work together to set the right pace for you.

Perhaps with a slight change in thinking, we can always enjoy the various seasons of life... *especially warming up the winter of life!*

PART 3

SOCIAL ISSUES

CHAPTER 17

LET ME CRIB IT ALL TONIGHT!

Is this what you sometimes feel like?.... CRY your heart out... Loud and clear, inattentive to who is around you and what they will think about you!

There comes a point in a few months or maybe a year or so when things look out of hand, and everything goes bizarre! Today, as I picked my diary, I felt same. Mood-off, feeling low, over-worked, things not going in the right direction, no one understands, no one helps, no one is concerned, no one ever seems willing to show any sympathy either... you feel all rotted! As if all the stars have conspired against you and will not show you any luck, come may whatever. The kids won't listen to you, the results go bad, they back answer, don't listen to me unless I shout... hubby & oldies are always preaching, but not helping, you don't have the time and patience to deal with tantrums of all kinds, and the list of drama never ends in life! You start feeling insane and you start doubting yourself if you have anger issues. The house that should have looked decorated around Diwali is messed up, the wardrobes are cluttered, the kitchen needs a stock up and intrinsic cleaning, the house and plants need your attention, toys are dropped on each nook & corner of the house, you feel like running away from all of this! Don't know where to start and how to end. Not even finding time for the freelancing work that you do! Gosh... sometimes life is cluttered like a garbage bin... even the mind needs a decluttering and even the phone looks burdened by the unending SMS and WhatsApp messages... And then you feel so exhausted by the burden of daily things that you don't feel capable of resolving all of this. Additionally, the maids & drivers go on a leave!!!

Then, since you have been raised and treated like a sophisticated, educated and courageous one, it's difficult to go off the league. BUT ... and mind it that this BUT is in capitals... But you want to break free for a while and speak your version of truth to all the selfish people in life. You also want to use all the abusive words you never used in your life and just ease yourself. It's not just the family, responsibilities, kids and overwork. When you see the newspaper or TV, see the people and hear about the stories in the society around you, you again feel charged due to crime injustice and inequality. The fraud, the murders, the psycho behavior of even the known people, all of it together makes you feel out of place! As if the world is not the right place to live for you! You hate things and you hate being fake as you are not speaking the truth in the face of people who deserve it. Maintaining the equations is not so easy. When things go wrong in your personal life, you start blaming yourself for not being able to handle things properly. The guilt sinks your heart, especially when you don't kiss your children saying goodnight in bed!

All the above said article saying 'you' is actually meant for 'me'. Too much cribbing I did it here... feeling better already! Otherwise, I will also read it aloud in the loneliness of my room before hitting the bed, though not feeling sleepy tonight... Mostly I also feel that it's the female gender that makes life like this... fully equipped but doing thankless jobs all the time!!! And always judged and criticized, in words or in ways to make you feel incapable or irrational!!!

All those who were responsible for my mood tonight, I will curse them right away and get rid of this rage, at least for now... and also this is the time that I pick up the diary to write down the to-do list starting tomorrow! I have to put everything in place- the house, the plants, the people around me, the timetable, and anything that is disturbing me! My decluttering mission starts this morning, so wish me luck, because I am sure many of you would be going through such a phase sometimes or even worse conditions to handle... so only you can understand my mood and my plight right now. Going to kiss my sleeping kids, and begin to repair my off-mood and fractured kind of life nowadays!

Thanks, Diary, CRIBBING in Writing is a super cool way to unwind !!! Goodnight!

CHAPTER 18

STORY OF ABUNDANCE: BREAKING THE SHACKLES

This is the story of a legal advisor, Shilpa and Vaibhav, an IT sector team leader, who were about to get married yesterday, but this afternoon they met in a cafe, and Shilpa called it OFF and walked away.

It was a shock for Vaibhav and his well-reputed family. Vaibhav had expected a nice first outing with her fiancée Shilpa. On the way to the cafe, he bought a beautiful red rose for her. He had hoped to ease her off any doubts regarding the last day, when his parents requested to cater to some expectations related to their son's wedding, but he not at all expected Shilpa to be so disturbed, as to call off the marriage. Vaibhav was on his bike, on his way to his home, thinking what the hell just happened!

Why couldn't he give her an equally rude response and break off the shackles from his side too? Why does he feel intimidated by the gesture of Shilpa? He recalled everything that happened that day. He called her up and asked her out for a coffee before she left the city with her parents, she agreed and said, even she wanted to meet him.

They met in the coffee house and placed an order for two coffees. She put out the jewellery box from her green tote bag and kept it on the table. Vaibhav looked at her unsure. She said that the last day made her doubtful regarding their compatibility and outlook towards life, so she wants to end it mutually, without any drama and hard feelings. Vaibhav insisted on the reason, which she said was the mental pressure they had created about the wedding and the expectations of DOWRY from it. It's not about being capable of giving it or not but about deciding the priorities and reasons to give it or not. And she was against the idea completely. DAHEJ in this form or other, was not a compromise for her and she was clear that she was not ready for a marriage with it. Vaibhav said he would talk to his parents regarding this, but Shilpa had made up her mind. For her marriage was not an obligation to be fulfilled, but a mutually agreed association for two compatible partners to live a better life, supporting each other in every walk of life. And with their poles-apart thoughts regarding dowry, it is not going to be sweet for a long time. Vaibhav felt the blame hard on his conscience!

He felt annoyed that he gave in to his parent's mentality about dowry. How could he not stand for himself that he was educated and working, and was capable enough to fulfil the needs of the house? Why was the house that father made still scantily furnished, though they had all the resources to furnish it tastefully? Why were they waiting for the bridal family to do it? He felt less manly. He knew he was capable of handling his expenses and also taking care of his future wife, even if she was not earning.

He remembered an alliance offer of that sweet & homely girl whom his family turned down as she was not earning. The girl was well-versed and talented and a great cook, and looked forward to her part of the contribution in every household affair, was that not still enough for Vaibhav? It was a series of incidents that flashed across his mind. It was not easy to handle rejection, and that too on a ground he was not comfortable with. He had a conscience after all. Everyone has a different situation, story and expectations from life. The difference lies in the thinking that we work in a way that we have enough for all of us to share as a family and live a comfortable and content life, and also offer a helping hand by contributing to others in society. Such thought leads to Abundance always... you will never feel a shortage of anything and work up towards self-improvement and growth. On the other hand, if we work in a way, thinking that we should grab the most out of life from anybody for ourselves, else others will benefit more from our loss, this indeed is a negative.

This is a mentality sure to always make you feel dwarfed. You may have a lot, but it's never enough. You have nothing to offer to others as your own needs are unfulfilled. You may feel yourself intelligent enough to snatch things from others by befooling or brainwashing them but such richness is never sustainable… it wipes you off and leaves you feeling like a beggar, obligated for the rest of your life. It will stop the possibility of self-improvement and growth in life. 'Dowry' this way or the other is the same nuisance of society! It will always leave its shadow on the relationship of a husband and a wife and the two families.

Vaibhav came home, straightaway went to his room and opened the Jewellery box to confirm that what had just happened was 'real'. And along with the chain and pendant that he had selected for Shilpa, he found a note from her, churning every bit of him. It said that she is not ready to move from Abundance to Scarcity. And that she chose a good life over a good alliance! Vaibhav could take it no longer. His mind was clear. He wanted to marry Shilpa, and no other woman could replace her. Her fierceness and clarity made her the partner of his dreams. He decided to sort this out and do the needful to win her back. He was sure of himself now. It took him two months to make things right.

> *He was a changed person. A more confident, honest and happy being, and perfect husband material. Shilpa was indeed going to be a lucky woman with this changed man. He would surely prove to be a man of her dreams!*

CHAPTER 19

STORY OF SCARCITY - DAHEJ, A TRADITION

When I was a kid, my granny used to tell me the story of two sisters - Sukhiya and Dukhiya. Sukhiya found a reason to be thankful for what she had and always remained happy, while Dukhiya always cried about what all she missed, things she did not have and cribbing of a tough life and stayed unhappy forever!

Now I know who the two sisters represented, Sukhiya was an Abundance Mindset while Dukhiya was a Scarcity Mindset. In life, every person can be categorized under these two mindsets. Ever heard that there is a currency crunch in every pocket and a room crunch in every house? That speaks of scarcity.

The house was bustling with giggles and activity. 'Nayi Bahu' was about to arrive. Before she entered her sasural, all the gifts of the wedding and 'Dahej' had already found a place in every nook and corner of the big house. It was a king-size teakwood designer bed with a side table, the dresser set placed in her new room and a five-door matching wardrobe! The room was adorned with new curtains, and the best available new technology 55" television was hanging on the front wall cabinet.

All was befitting for the arrival of 'Nayi Bahu', it looked as if the lifestyle of the family had changed overnight. The drawing room had a huge set of 7-seater L-shaped sofas, curated for the space and a marble top centre table. The dining room had an 8-seater arrangement with a glass-top dining table set and teakwood chairs. The cutlery, the dinner set, the dazzling stainless steel cooking utensils... the list looked hard to capture. The newness of the house made it enormous as everything that entered into it adorned and occupied it.

It was nothing that Vaibhav or 'his family' had asked for, it was a gift from 'ladki wale' for the love of their daughter, Shilpa. After all Vaibhav's father had built a big house and he was the only son to enjoy living in it. Vaibhav worked in the IT sector and earned well. His only sister was six years older than him and married off to an engineer working in the government sector, posted in another city. Shilpa was told about her good luck by friends and relatives from the time the wedding bells started tinkling. It was an arranged marriage, and the word 'Dahej' cannot be skipped here, isn't it?

For Shilpa, she was a well-educated, well-versed, multitalented girl of the modern era. She also worked as a legal expert for a reputed firm, earning well. But since she was supposed to marry and move to another city, she had to temporarily leave her job and look for opportunities, later on, in the new city where she would live with Vaibhav and his family. On her first meeting with Vaibhav, he told her that he didn't want any 'dowry' and was against the idea… BUT would not hurt the feelings of his parents who had spent so much on him on his education and bringing up, also they will be living in the huge house made by his father, so should respect their 'hopes' with the marriage of their only son!

Additionally, they had not saved a penny while marrying off his elder sister. As her groom was a government employee, his parents were overwhelmed imagining the beautiful future of their daughter 'Vrisha' and had offered everything from cash to kind, for the expenses of the wedding and every bit of furnishing of their home and a car for the 'Vidaii' ceremony. So, now it's the turn of their son's wedding, and how could he be insensitive towards them? !!! And being the only son, doesn't he have the responsibility to look after his old-aged parents?

Shilpa was devastated as the voices screamed inside her - Didn't my parents spend on educating me and looking after me for bringing up? Don't I live in a house made by 'my' parents? And that house I am told to leave forever, for the sake of marriage and live with you and your family? Don't I earn well and do great in my career, that I have to take a break and may or may not be able to start afresh in a new city, for the sake of this marriage? And you talk about the only son... what about my family 'who has just two daughters and NO son', are they supposed to suffer and pay forever for the conventions of this 'sick mentality' of society?

Doesn't 'she' have the responsibility to look after her parents in their old age, just because she is a daughter and not a son??? Was she not supposed to decide how and where to spend her income, and on whom, just because she got married? WHY on earth are the bride's parents considered full of 'abundance' to keep giving away to the groom's family, who is always in SCARCITY and yearning for the wedding to happen and keeping their house empty for the 'Nayi Bahu' to fill in? She was so full of anger and pain, that she chose to keep 'quiet' for the time being!

Shilpa and Vaibhav had met through a matrimonial site and instantly liked each other on the initial interaction and chatting. But just when their parents met for the sake of the wedding, this 'dahej' version of Vaibhav and his parents made her restless! Vaibhav's father said that they have a big house, but they would want it to be furnished as per her 'bahu's' choice, so her parents can take up on the project. Vaibhav's mother had said that 'Jewellery

& gifts' from the bride's home are a matter of pride in their society, so nothing more, just to keep up with the traditions and do the needful.

On the phone and chatting, Vaibhav had told her that he was of modern thoughts and believed in equality. That he liked independent women earning on their own, and though 'they' might have to make adjustments for the sake of staying together after the wedding, she won't find a problem working, even after marriage. He had said that he is against 'dowry' though his parents might not be of the same mentality, and follow a traditional approach.

Since a lot had been discussed over the phone and parents had a word on the phone too, so it was pre-decided that if all looked good upon meeting, they would finalise the wedding. Shilpa's parents wanted her happiness, she had spoken highly of Vaibhav... they agreed to the alliance! They put a gold chain on Vaibhav... and he had himself chosen a beautiful pendant in an intricate gold chain to adorn her fiancée Shilpa.

It was the next day afternoon they met in a cafe before Shilpa left the city with her parents to come back again only as a bride. She spoke her mind to Vaibhav over the cup of coffee for them that 'SHE' paid for. She handed over the Jewellery box ' with the chain & pendant' and a note that said :

> *"SCARCITY is a mentality. With all you have in life, you still don't have enough and so you want others to fulfil it for you! I am NOT ready to move from ABUNDANCE to SCARCITY. I rather choose a good life over a good alliance. No grudges, wish you a good life ahead!"*

Exactly TWO months of Vaibhav's apologies, and an arrangement where the couple financially shared to furnish the house together, on EMI's, and vowed to look after both *'the set of parents'* equally, for the rest of their lifetime as responsible children, the wedding date was announced. Shilpa's parents were happy and proud of the 'audacity' and *'sanskar'* their daughter exhibited in such a scenario and gave justice to the education she got. They knew they could afford the *'dahej'* they were asked for, but the new generation has taken over such obligations!

They willingly insisted and gifted the shining blue car to the newly wedded couple *to start a new journey with comfort and luxury... for Shilpa's Vidaii from their home of abundance!*

CHAPTER 20

REVEAL: DON'T INSTIGATE ME

Some things are best hidden inside, like our anger, hurt, revenge and the worst face of us. Bringing it out will either end it for good or bring turbulence which might be hard to handle and ruin things further.

Meet the best of the Sadhu-Sant or the motivational speakers and gurus, and ask them if they 'never' felt anger. For any human being, it's natural to experience 'human emotions' like desire, greed, anger, need, frustration, love, hate, empathy, sympathy, need, helplessness, hope and the list is long. But we tend to keep things in control, to the best we can.

Excess of anything is bad. I am an Aries soul and just like a newborn baby… it hardly takes me any time to turn from level one of emotional intensity to the danger zone in any of the traits, I have. I am frank, possessive and cheerful, but when triggered to my limits may end up being rude, and aggressive due to insecurity and sometimes thoughtlessness about consequences. Once I ended up holding the collar of one sick molester and giving a tight slap on his face publicly... he was way bigger in body & age. My courage and adventurous nature, often make me impulsive and accident-prone, indulging in risky situations. Being too straightforward is also very dangerous in the Indian scenario of handling household and relationships, but somehow people around me have adjusted to my mood swings and fairytale lifestyle.

I am hopelessly optimistic, honest, ambitious and hardworking, but at the same time, if instigated I may become ruthless and unsympathetic to my enemies and opponents. If they put a hurdle in my way, I will make sure that their way is full of spines... I am revengeful! And I like myself the way I am... Being good to good ones, being a villain to those who ask for it by their deeds..! I am also a romantic... passionate lover, loyal and giving... and very jealous, but secret conditions apply! And though it's becoming too much of a revelation, it's mandatory to put it straight that I don't interfere in others' arena unless it somehow disturbs my peace of mind or I am being called for help. I am a confident decision-maker, and quite proud of having clarity of mind. I respect others' points of view and don't judge them without giving them a fair chance, but I also don't allow anyone to be unreasonable to me... so kindly keep a safe distance depending on my moodiness!

One additional revelation, this thought has been hovering over me for some time now... and it's a sure shot way to know your hidden feelings about a person or situation. Ever imagined, what would happen if you good hear the inner voices of each other? I am sure the idea thrills... It's a bit Scary, isn't it? We human beings makeup and present speech in a way too refined state. Not that it means that our thoughts are 'always' evil, but for sure it is 'too raw' to be pleasant enough for any ears. The choice of words is altered too of what we think versus what we say. Even if one day this happens, we could hear each other's inner voice, then the world will be a changed place, and all equations will be different. One may hear many slang and truths, and may vent out way too much even to imagine! Personally, sometimes I tend to lose the perfect balance of words and such diplomacy and become way too straightforward, to be surely mistaken or maybe rightly taken as rude, arrogant and high-headed.

Having said and revealed a lot many things about me, let me act like a kind and considerate friend of you and a no-nonsense lady, unless you instigate me! And let me stick to my mantra of 'writing more- speaking less' and believing in this quote by an American Fashion Designer Rachel Zoe:

"Style is a way to say who you are, without having to speak." I think I am way too stylish as well!

Okay, putting an end to this liberty of boasting off, off the limits... unless you instigate me again by putting up such a prompt!

CHAPTER 21

CONCEAL – THE REAL-LIFE NIGHTMARE!

Past few days my maid 'Rani' has been acting weird. She was not her usual self-chattering every news of the entire universe. Right now she was just sneaking in, doing her work, leaving in haste and making no eye contact.

I asked her if there was something wrong, but she said nothing. Such are the evils of society that even when it's needed, people are more concerned about their reputation rather than asking for help.

Later in the evening, I learnt from my other maid who cooks, that Rani's daughter 'Rupa' had been found! Found, as in... was she missing? I could not understand... then came this hard-to-believe story that Rani herself confided to me the next day! She looked relieved that her daughter was back home. Rupa was about 14-15 years old, she went out to buy something from the grocery store nearby and then was missing the past three days. Scared of ruining the family reputation and with the elder daughter's marriage proposal at stake, they searched everywhere on their own and never informed the police. Rather they told everyone around that she had gone to the village to her grandmother's place.

And after three days, she walked back home, in a shunned state. Her family put her in a room, not let anyone meet her for many days. Rupa was not answering queries and just said that she couldn't remember details, and she was given some medicine that she felt drowsy all the time... what she could recollect was that she was made to wear a chunri over her head, covering her face and blindfolded & handcuffed, then taken to some place in an auto and local train. She was kept in a dark room for three days, and two men visited the room to molest her and would leave. She was being drugged regularly. After the ordeal, again in the same way, they left her on the local train, and somehow when she gathered her senses, she came home.

No case was filed, no action was taken, nor anyone looked at all keen on finding the culprit. I asked Rani, what if Rupa didn't come back? Wouldn't you have taken any action to find her? She was taken aback but was clear in her mind, "Didi, ek ladki ke karan baki sabko nahi chhor sakte hain na... humlog ka pareshani aur badh jayega... ab jo kismat me hoga wo jhelna hi parega!" She made it clear that there is no merit in knowing about her whereabouts anymore, and soon when things settle a bit, she will get 'her daughter' married and this episode will be over for life. They were clueless about the culprit, or this is what she told me. And if Rupa wouldn't have returned, they would have left her to destiny.

Meanwhile, what kind of physical, mental and emotional trauma she might have gone through in those three days of being CAPTIVE is beyond anyone's imagination. The nightmare was OVER for her and the family, at least what they showed up. The three dark days for Rupa would be CONCEALED forever, from the family's discussion and society's gossip. They felt thankful that she was not murdered or sold off and that she was alive... doesn't matter what she went through already! Probably, that sounds logical and is the most practical and basic thing considered in the decision of CONCEALING it forever... I am sometimes dumbfounded to see the kind of society we live in... where the plight of females is to struggle or compromise or die!

Sometimes, my Nani's words echo in my mind, 'Girls are beautiful beings and appear as a blessing... till the time they are saved from real-life ordeals! And for that reason, I feel saved from such trauma to see my daughters in pain of in-numerous kinds, when a boy is born!' I wonder if it's a CURSE, to be born as a female. Be it a well-to-do class of people or the uneducated & less privileged ones, the lifestyle changes, but the plight is the same for females...

Struggle - for existence, for choice of the kind of life you want to lead, and for living your OWN life;

Compromise every day with the norms of society and traditions, which surely are gender specific and male-dominant;

OR *Die* - the easiest way out of this place, still the way you die & suffering would be decided by the culprits, you might get extremely unlucky!

And then we celebrate *'being Women'* the most beautiful creation of God... *Cheers to that!*

CHAPTER 22

THE ADDICT

The problem with addiction is that it doesn't just kill an ADDICT. It rather kills the family, the kids and all those who tried their best to help!!! Here's a story, based on true incidents we often see around.

*I*t was a group video call, and the three of them connected often… Menka, Meera & Madhavi. Madhavi let her inhibitions go and cried bitterly. Life had been unfair for her in many ways, and she often wondered why she had to go through so many struggles. She had always been brave… once when her mother died in an accident leaving behind the two sisters, not even teenagers, long for mother's love forever. Then they survived the shock when their father married again, left the two daughters with maternal grandparents, and broke all bonds forever. She encouraged herself that her maternal family took good care of the two sisters, which was a blessing. Also when Madhavi found support of family to study in a good school and become a graduate. But she never got an opportunity to have a career, and she accepted the wish of her maternal family where she grew up. She had an early marriage to an eligible bachelor Rakesh, working as a junior officer in the Air Force, and she was happy with her fate then. Rakesh was a loving and caring husband, and life looked good for a long time. They had a son, Ranjay, a bright active kid. But past ten years or so, life took a drastic turn. Madhavi was lately dealing with an 'alcoholic' husband and his newly found extramarital affair, that almost broke her.

"Don't you understand girl, he is an 'addict'… your expectations of love, loyalty, responsibility and whatever was from your 'sane' husband, not an addict…! And addiction does qualify as a brain disease… it's a compulsive behaviour that you need to fight and cure… and that starts with ACCEPTING that HE IS AN ADDICT - A patient of Addiction!!!

But I am afraid for you my dear friend… because your addiction to 'him' now seems more dangerous than his addiction to 'alcohol'!" said Meera, aghast discussing the same thing again and again, every time, for so many years now.

It was a team of three besties… and with their own share of achievements and problems in life. They have been together since school days. Holding each other in the ups

The Addict

and downs of life, just being there 'emotionally' if not in any other way… But this friendship alone provided them with a lot of joy in good times and strength during the struggles.

Menka intercepted, "Cry… cry it out today, never to cry again. We are here to support you in every way we can. But practically, it's YOUR life, and ONLY you can take steps to make it your way!!!"

It was clearly visible that Madhavi was caught in a vicious circle, and was not able to break it for a long time now. Isn't it the same thing with addiction? ADDICTION TO A PERSON !!! She wanted to but could neither stop caring for her husband nor live with him peacefully. She would not let him go, nor would she stop fighting her lungs out, and the situation was worsening with every passing day.

What once had been a lovey-dovey pair about a decade ago, now turned out to be an abusive stressful household story, conducive to none… neither Madhavi, nor her husband Rakesh, and a mental trauma for their only son Ranjay. Ranjay was such a bright student that even with limited means and resources, and a never-ending family drama at home, he was a school topper in 10th boards. He was the hope for his mother, and she loved him. But she was not able to free herself from Rakesh for various reasons… first it was her undying love that still existed, how so ever harsh words she used for him, and secondly, the finances... practically a major factor. Even though Rakesh was an alcoholic and an addict, he was the only earning member and did provide money for the needs of his family. The sad part was that he threatened to stop the money for the household and his son's studies if they did not allow him his freedom from alcohol & extramarital affairs... and Madhavi couldn't find the strength and confidence to deal with this. She gave in to such abuse and mental torture, and was living with it only to move towards a state of 'depression'.

Meera & Menka were well aware of her emotional state and were worried at the same time. Staying in different cities, it was not easy to keep track of the everyday situation, though they made it a point to consciously keep in touch and fuel Madhavi with some motivation. But as the saying goes, God only helps those, who help themselves! Madhavi was so caught in this viscous circle, that she lost her mind to the level of addict. She would repeat what bad Rakesh did, which in her opinion was so mean and unfair... and kept comparing herself with the woman Rakesh had fallen for. She would keep checking their calls & messages, and the expenses Rajesh did on his new love. After knowing about the affair, her focus was not on Rakesh being an alcoholic... but only on how could he cheat on her... and this was only leading to

The Addict

more stress, ugly fights, and arguments to demean and hurt each other, worsening things to a point of no return.

Meera & Menka suspected that the full family was in a state of self-harm, and were trying hard to make Madhavi look at her state from an outsider's view, that she needed to break free of the shackles of negative emotions and work practically to save her family. They are still trying to reach out to her, and will never leave her hand. (Meanwhile, they seek advice from all of you too.)

Dear Madhavi,

Read this, whenever you feel low and scared. Please open your heart and mind when you read this… We have been friends since childhood, and we feel each other's joy and pain like no one else! We LOVE you… Different from the families we live in, we share a close bond of FRIENDSHIP that's comparable to no relationship tags… And we can't imagine a life without YOU. You are part of our daily thoughts and prayers, even if we don't talk daily. So, here is what we want you to try and understand… for the good of all.

We had accepted Rakesh as a part of you when you got married to him and were happy. But the person you married, no longer exists in that form… he is now an ADDICT. Simply put, an Addict is a person who doesn't have control over doing, taking or using something to the point where it could be harmful to oneself and others.

Rakesh is an alcoholic now and for a long time now. We know you tried hard, and are still trying. You tried to put him in REHABILITATION many times, but he returned with fury for you. You tried to convince him with your love, but he only fooled around. He has lost his senses to respond to your confrontation. He is getting abusive to your only son. You both are creating such a lasting 'ugly' memory for your son, he surely doesn't deserve this. All your best efforts are done. But things are not working for good. It has been a lot more than enough for your suffering now, and the kid you have given birth to.... deserves your love, care and protection... and a better life indeed!

With your son, Ranjay in view, it's in the best interest of all that you try something different that works for your own good. You have to gather all your scattered thoughts and energy, and become the lady of strength... You have to move out of your shell. You have to think logically and work practically. Stop focusing on Rakesh and 'his' life, it no longer holds any good for you... start building YOURSELF. Get your fears fly away, and save the precious things that are still intact in your life. Your education needs your attention, as it wants to aid you in finding ways to EARN for yourself and end your dependency on your 'alcoholic' husband.

Your family & friends, your son, the everyday people who support you in one way or another in dealing with

The Addict

household abuse, we stand by you and will support you in every way we can. But you do have to take the first step, you have to break the shackles, and you have to strive to create a beautiful life for you and your son. Work towards making memories of the present, worth remembering in the future. Ignore the ADDICT, his presence and his futile drama around you that just intends to create pain. You are stronger than him, and you have to prove to yourself that YOU ARE NOT A VICTIM… YOU ARE NOT ADDICTED TO his abuse and any EMOTIONS towards him, except, if at all it should be KINDNESS towards a PATIENT.

Get yourself out of this mess, MOVE ON !!!

We LOVE you. Life is a gift, that we must enjoy and also make it worthwhile. It's precious, not to be spent on LOST cause! We are waiting to see a NEW BEGINNING for you… Time is ticking, it's time to act.

With Best Wishes,

Menka & Meera

CHAPTER 23

CURSE: MARRIED TO A MONSTER IN DISGUISE

Sulekha had a lonely childhood as she lost her mother at a very young age when she was still in primary school. But his father took charge of both his kids: Sulekha and her 4-year elder brother Siddharth. He did everything in his capacity to look after them and raise them as educated and responsible adults. Sulekha studied law and joined a law firm, while Siddharth started a business after graduating and was doing well in that. He also got married to a girl named Sonia, and it looked like a good life.

Sulekha confided in her bhabhi and told her about how her "friendship" turned into an affair with Anshu, who lived nearby in the same colony. Anshu was good-looking and educated and was trying his luck in competitive exams to become an officer. He needed time to settle, but he wasn't in a rush because he was also earning money from the rental of family property. She requested her bhabhi to put this up to her father and Siddharth in a befitting manner. But her bhabhi had other plans. She was worried about expenses for Sulekha's wedding and also that Sidd would spend lavishly on her only sister. She wanted to delay it, at least. So, the way she disclosed the matter to the family caused anger and disturbance in the relationship between Sulekha and his brother and father. They did not consent to her marriage to Anshu, who was not yet established, though he belonged to an affluent family.

Sulekha was in emotional wreck, knowing how "Sonia Bhabhi" had purposefully put on such a show, having no support from her brother or father, and even Anshu was unsettled and growing frustrated by the day. After denial in her family, even Anshu was showing a changed attitude towards her, blaming her for saying she didn't want to marry him. In her heart, Sulekha had this guilt that if she did not marry Anshu due to family pressure, she would be blamed for being selfish and leaving in his time of need, as he was unsettled, for her entire life. Not out of love, but of guilt, she decided to marry Anshu, even against the will of her family. It was a court marriage. It was against the wishes of both families. Nobody but common friends were a witness. Anshu's family had a wish for a better looking... should say 'gori, Sundar, Sushil, grih karya me nipun' kind of sanskari 'not-working' bahu... which Sulekha didn't fit. But as soon as she came home after the wedding with Anshu, she was curtly told that if she continued her job, she would have to give her salary to the family, aka her MIL, who manages the home. Also, since her husband was jobless, she had to support him too by bearing his expenses. Sulekha was somehow aware that things were not moving in the right direction, but she was clueless about what was yet to come.

Three years later, Sulekha was in a hospital to get her injuries and hand fractures treated. A friend accompanied her to the hospital. No one from Mayeka or Sasural was concerned about her plight. Her drunkard husband hit her. He grabbed her hand and threw her out of the house at midnight. The reason doesn't even matter here. She was still the only earning member of the household. Yet it was Anshu who was so naive to have fallen for her (a wicked girl who tricked him!) that he could not clear any competitive exams. Sulekha also had to furnish the in-laws' house because her family had not given her anything for the wedding, and she was doing it slowly.

Additionally, after her full-time job, she was unable to devote the "expected" time to household work even though she cooked the meals in the morning before leaving and dinner after coming back. So that's a lot of reason to get hit by a drunken husband, isn't it? Her bhabhi, Sonia, had prohibited her from entering their house since the day she got married to Anshu.

Sulekha's father came to meet her when she was hit initially in the first year of her marriage, to sympathise and forgive her, and the best he suggested was to ask for forgiveness and try to compromise with her "chosen husband." This time, when he visited Sulekha in the hospital, he advised her to decide for herself and the toddler she had given birth to. But her father was too old and weak to support her anymore. He was made dependent for everything on his son and daughter-in-law. Sulekha felt numb. Lonely. She missed her mother like never before. What she could vaguely remember about her mother was that she found strength in her words and her arms. She decided to stand up for herself and not be a victim anymore.

Other than the law firm, she had also joined a school as a student counsellor and psychologist. She was earning well. She was caring for her toddler son on her own and had enrolled him in the same school where she worked. Her son was his lifeline now. She didn't want to see fear and pain in his eyes. She didn't want his childhood to be jeopardized because of her weakness in remaining in a failed marriage. And she didn't want her son to witness her mother beaten like a nobody... and then cry for her! She had no strings to keep attached to her 'mayeka' or Sasural. Her father sometimes came to meet her, and that was all.

Right from the hospital, she called the police to file a complaint of domestic violence against her husband and called her courtroom friends for legal procedure. She filed for divorce. She also found a room to stay with her son and moved in with "nothing" but her personal belongings that she collected from her "so-called home" under police protection.

It was a new beginning. Out of all the horrifying memories of rudeness and ruthlessness! A beautiful new journey, free from all obligations, with the one person she loved and the one who loved her back in multiples, her son...

She named him "Dhruv"—"the one shining star in the darkest of nights!"

CHAPTER 24

REACH OUT, BEFORE THE DEATH ON DIAGONAL LANE

What do we normally do when we hear the sounds of hue and cry from our neighborhood? What do we do when we see a couple fighting and calling names to each other on the street, outside a small dwelling place?

*D*o we ever think that we should interfere as a society, when we hear the sounds of abuse from the near by flat in an apartment? Even if we find a husband and wife in a fit of physical violence with each other, to wound the spouse physically, do we try to stop them?

'Domestic Violence' is one of the most talked about scenario in today's world as women are getting more vocal about it than earlier, still the least interfered one by the society. In all the above scenarios, 'we' as a society mostly label it as a 'couple thing' or 'a personal matter of husband and wife' and excuse ourselves from it. But is it the right thing to do? Won't you feel the guilt of not saving someone, somewhere, which gave a glimpse of disturbance to you just a few days ago. It was a fit of anger... and an unrevealed story of this unfortunate family that met death on the diagonal lane!

Story 1 -

A handsome young businessman shot his 2 year old son, his beautiful young wife and then ended himself too putting the bullet in his head. It was the talk of the town for a few days. Many stories were curated by the local newspapers, about the constant sounds of quarrel heard almost daily by the neighbors (who chose not to do anything, nor interfere in a couple fight) though the truth was buried with the death of the couple. It might be a story of distrust or betrayal, an emotional crisis. It was said that the wife was involved in an affair that the husband came to know about and killed her in a fit of rage.

Story 2 -

The couple were in a financial crisis, and the were unable to find a solution to it, so in depression and blaming each other for a ruined life they often fought (uninterrupted by the society as it's husband-wife thing). One evening, the wife hung herself, and the husband was arrested as a suspect for causing this incident. But what surfaced as a word of mouth finally was that the reason was a drunkard husband who could not cater to household needs financially and also led to physically abuse his wife under the affect of alcohol... 'Domestic Violence'.

Story 3-

This is a story of a modern educated working woman, who also looked after the financial needs of her matrimonial family including in-laws, yet was subjected to extreme physical, mental, verbal abuse by the full family including her husband, who could not land into a decent job and was insulted by his own family. After struggling and living with the abuse for more than five years, she finally saved herself from death by moving out of the house with the help of police and her friends, and got a divorce. (But the torment of the society, and moral lectures of her own family, still continues.) Is Domestic Violence a shame for the victim? What kind of mindset is that of our society?

Story 4-

This newly married woman was not allowed to meet her own parents and family after marriage. She was not allowed to mingle with anyone, not even neighbours. She was kept aloof for three years under different scenarios and was just used as domestic help in the name of marriage. She slowly lost her senses and got mentally disturbed. Her parents had to take charge because of suspicion, and got her out of the house with legal help, once she was out of touch even on phone for more than two months or so. Later, it was found that the family wanted to hide the husband's impotency and 'black magic practices' prevalent in their family, for which they found this woman as a scapegoat to continue being scene normal in the eyes of society. The 'divorce case' is still going on in the court, while the woman is treated for her mental instability acquired in past 3 years of marriage.

The list of stories of domestic violence is countless and the types of abuse is beyond our scariest imagination. But what rings a bell in all the above said scenarios is that 'we' the people - the family, friends, neighbours- we are failing as a society by not doing our duty as responsible citizens and human beings. We are saving our faces in the name of 'personal matter' and 'couple fight' and 'family drama' or whatever words we can frame to get rid of unnecessary trouble.

Instead, if we take charge and as a community we chose to interfere in matters which are "being heard out of the walls of the house" and can no longer be called 'personal', some life may be saved. Some quarrel may be ended or resolved. Some lessons may be learnt by the people involved. If it's beyond the norms of humanity, informing the police or women cell or child welfare committee or the Lok Adalat might be the most important step taken to save a victim from a possible threat on life. Resident Welfare Associations should be created and societies should put members in it from legal or police or NGO background, to whom people may reach out in case of requirement. Social activities and meetings should be encouraged, so that aloofness of human beings doesn't turn into unreported crimes. People should also be made aware of such crimes and about the law as that we have in our country to fight it.

Some Laws that deal with domestic violence cases are given below as follows:

1. **Protection of Women Against Domestic Violence Act, 2005** - A law passed by Indian Parliament to safeguard women against domestic violence including economic, physical, emotional, sexual, verbal abuse; save them from men and relatives of the family etc in a married or even a live-in relationship.
2. **The Dowry Prohibition Act, 1961** - The criminal code that punishes by imprisonment and fine, for the give and take or even the demand of dowry or gift.
3. **Section 498A IPC-** A criminal law that applies to spouse or husband's relatives who are cruel to woman or harass her for dowry or abuse her in any form

forcing her to suicide or putting her life and Heath under risk etc

When it was said that 'man is a social animal' it carried a huge meaning and inference of it... most visible and needful in today's world of insensitiveness towards happenings in other's life. Not interfering in others business is good only as long as it doesn't cross the boundaries of humanity. Else a human being standing for supporting and saving another human being in need, is the only essence of being human, isn't it? This is good for thought...

I hope and wish to see more solutions to such social issues in the coming years. Till then, I believe spreading awareness and taking action to save life of someone in need, about to die in the diagonal lane, would only make us feel more human. ***Reach out to help someone in need, say 'NO' to Domestic Violence!!!***

PART 4

LIFE & DEATH

CHAPTER 25

STYLE UP: YOUR SEALED LIPS!

"Style is a way to say who you are, without having to speak."

– **Rachel Zoe**

*W*elcome to the Society of Sealed Lips...! We are a society where most of the things are known to each one, but we are too 'ashamed' to talk about it. If not ashamed, we may be 'bound' by traditions, not to speak up and show such audacity. Also, we shouldn't speak in between when two elders are talking. Shouldn't utter a word about the family issues in the society, whether it be domestic violence or even a gruesome crime happening in there. And if you are a female, you shouldn't speak when the brainy species of males are having a word with each other... But let me not sound like a gender-biased feminist and also mention that if a household or family issue is being discussed by the females, it is best said that *'auraton ke* *mamle me mat paro!*', even if it's a crucial issue requiring to solve in the capacity of family. Age might bring a lot of experience, but does it mean that all aged people talk sense? Are they all so knowledgeable and clean, that you shouldn't dare to argue at all... and sorry, I forgot... you should keep your mouth just shut!!!

There may be thousands of other reasons and excuses to keep your lips pinned, for the safety of 'social norms'! So, a safety pin came to our rescue, like in the prompt: 'Ek chup, Sau Sukh... or Maybe hazaar dukh?' But there comes a time in life when you break the rules. It comes with a hope. A hope to overcome the fear and pain. To be free of succumbing to the dark insides. To speak up! Let the world label you whatsoever... it can't be worse than keeping the suffering to yourself and dying a thousand deaths...! So, I thought maybe we plant a seed of hope and see how this seed grows for a better society. And here is what it led me to imagine. Most of the New Year wishes or wishes for a new beginning start with the word "Hope".

For example:

- "Hope this year is better than last year."
- "Hope it's not as bad as last year."
- "Hope things get better and back to the "usual normal" this year... and so on."

But there are several other hopes, that we hardly speak about. The most relatable example in this Covid time would be the situation that, once your friend or relative gets unwell, you say, "Hope you get well soon." But you continue to start hoping secretly too…Something like "Hope that others don't catch an infection from you. Hope it is not Covid. Hope he is not hiding his true symptoms. Hope we maintained a safe distance from the infected last time we met there." It is nothing bad that you hope, but it might not be pleasant enough for the suffering person to hear it straight, isn't it? That led me to a strange idea that follows.

What would happen if you could hear the inner voice of others? I am sure the idea thrills… But would it be okay if your inner voice could be heard by others too? Scary, isn't it? We human beings makeup and present speech in a way too refined state. Not that it means that our thoughts are 'always' evil, but for sure it is 'too raw' to be pleasant enough for any ears. The choice of words is altered too of what we think versus what we say. Even if one day this happens, we could hear each other's inner voice, then the world will be a changed place, and all equations will be different. One may hear many slang and truths, and may vent out way too much even to imagine!

Personally, sometimes I tend to lose the perfect balance of words and such diplomacy and become way too straightforward, to be surely mistaken or maybe rightly taken as rude, arrogant and high-headed. But probably in the same scenario, if we speak our minds, if we ease out our vows if we clear out the intentions and anger, much of the hidden abusers will come out on the surface. The society might turn into a jungle, with all sophistication lost, but at least the innocent would be saved from the predators. So, in my view, it's important to make yourself, your guts, your anger, your Yes or NO known to society... now it's up to you and your wits... also it's up to your courage that you do it by speaking up RAW or show it in your fervour that you are not a NOBODY to be taken as the one with 'sealed lips'!

STYLE it ladies... buck up and let's stand in solidarity for each other... After all, is it not 'solidarity' that the 'safety pin' on our 'sealed lips' stands for?

CHAPTER 26

IGNITE THE DURGA IN YOU

Yes, she is a woman... Mostly peaceful, loving, caring, sharing and supporting the lives of near and dear ones, until SHE is 'ignited'... and it takes just a spark to see her fuming... ready to consume all that comes in her way, to protect those in her shelter... Because SHE is DURGA and yes, the Durga lives within me!!!

In her shelter lies her children, whom she so bravely protects and so lovingly nourishes to support them in growing up... if in danger, she will no longer stick to traditions and rules, she will consume the ones in the rage and fire, anyone who threatens the safety of her children. SHE teaches her young children to be alert and safe from the demons who might be masked. Those lurking eyes on the road, if it discomforts you, it's a demon. Even if it's a senior or a teacher or any authority who calls you alone in a corner, if it feels wrong to you, say NO... it might be a demon, and you don't have to be scared of it, because I am with you and will protect you always. If it's a driver or a stranger who signals you inappropriately, shout or stop that demon, or hide to be safe, or run away if you have to... act sensibly but never feel alone, as I am your mother, and will always protect you of demons, I will stand with you always!

In her shelter lies the love and respect for close ones who matter to her- be it her parents, her siblings, her spouse, a close friend, a colleague, a relative, a neighbor, or even a stranger child who holds her heart by his cuteness... She will be ignited if anyone in her vicinity is harmed by a modern-day demon. Be it disrespectful behavior shown towards the old parents, be it a distrust shown by a boss to your spouse, be it a complaint about the grades deteriorating for your child, be it a colleague entangled in a relationship crisis, be it your relative in a financial crunch, or a stranger child beaten by an insensitive parent, be it her sibling tortured by the in-laws... the DURGA is ignited. She will not leave a stone unturned to take control of the situation and ease you out of the danger of loss. She will protect you and your life. She will be there, as your friend, a guide, a mentor, a sister, a wife, a daughter, a protector... in her grace, her aura, a hell of a woman... to protect you from the demons!

In her shelter also lies the virtues of a woman that she so dearly holds, that when thrashed, she will be ignited. It's her self-respect, that you dare not crush. It's her sanctity, that you better don't doubt. It's her love for you, but you must not take her for granted. It's her sacrifice for the sake of family and kids, you must know she is not weak and unworthy. It's her freedom of life, that you must not challenge. It's her way of living, you are not obliged to judge. Because I told you, let the Durga in her stay peaceful... and don't flash the spark to ignite it... Else once she ignites, she will rest only when the demons are demolished and the ones in her shelter are safe under her protection!!!

Dear Woman,

Never be scared, instead let the world be wary of your hidden powers... yes, the Durga resides in each one of us. Do Ignite the Durga in You, when need be... society needs us in all our avatars... make it safe for all those in our shelter, from the unseen unknown disguised and masked demons all around!!!

The Durga in YOU... The Durga is YOU!

CHAPTER 27

WEAKNESS – THE LAST DIARY ENTRY

Hello Diary,

*T*oday is my daughter's birthday. *If she was alive, she would have been quitting the teens...* completed 19 years and going on 20... I am sure she would have grown into a beautiful and strong woman if she lived. But I somehow killed her when I couldn't prove myself strong enough to protect her. I could not educate her on how to 'endure and survive', neither did I teach her to be 'strong enough and live life'!

Diary, you are the one and only one I can open up. This is the last time I pour my heart to you before I die. I don't want to address it to anybody else. If anyone mattered to me, or I had a worthy place in their life, I wouldn't have opted for a lifeless you! I am too fed up with life. Life has become nothing more than a mundane everyday routine, and in the breaks, it's just tears, guilt, regret, anger and never-ending pain. Yes, I sound depressed, and I have every reason to be like this. Today I want to recollect my whole life before I end it for good.

I thank God for the beautiful childhood I had. I still have glimpses of a young myself, running around and playing with friends, laughing my heart out and shouting to be heard... falling while riding a bicycle, cooing my pet dog, travelling with my family, hugs of my mother, affection of my father, giggling with my sister and everything was so perfect. The only beautiful phase of my life I had. I am 41 years old now. I suffered a bad marriage that ruined everything for me and my family. Things never got better, however hard I tried.

In the first place, it was domestic abuse. I could have dealt with it in a better way, but probably I was immature at that time and didn't dare to stand up against a demon who would torture me in every way and without a break. I sometimes lay beaten, bleeding, faint... felt as if I was about to die... but it was not enough. In the course, my parents got involved and put up police complaints that worked against me. In the context of a better life, I was lured to another city... and the domestic abuse came back into the picture. I had no courage, I had given up on physical pains and wished that I rather get killed.

My parents were far away and if at all I talked to them sometimes, I knew they were quite old and struggling with health issues. I stopped bothering them, though I knew they were not at peace, with my plight. Plus they had other two children, to look after. Probably my depression was reaching out to them somehow and killing them bit by bit, making them feel helpless! And then I got pregnant.

The domestic abuse 'got less' for a few years, or maybe I adjusted to it somehow as my focus was turned to my baby. It was a girl, she was an angel to me who took away my wrath and gave me the courage to go on, for her sake. The demon accepted her when she was still small, but years gone, I saw chains restricting her life that I was not happy about. The chain of obligations as a female... how to behave in this unjust society and unfair world.

She turned 17 years old, going on 18...two years back. A girl full of life and laughter, my younger self, happy and healthy. She was 'seen' with a male friend by his father, who got angry. His demon instinct came back and he hit my girl. I tried and save her from the monster but probably the hurt was done elsewhere, on her heart and soul. I consoled her while she sobbed in her room that evening. I made her eat a 'Roti' somehow and put her to sleep. And she slept. And never woke up. The next morning we found her hanging on the ceiling fan. My baby, my angel, my everything... my younger self, my love... she was gone forever! She left a suicide note, saying,

> *'I love you maa... but I don't want to suffer like you, just because I am born a girl. And I don't want to see you in tears anymore! You endured a lot, but I wish you were stronger. Please forgive me, but I feel the same weakness in me, just like you. If I can't fight for the right, I will have a hell of a life like you. You will cry for me maa. But I can't live in chains. I will better end it now.'*

For the past two years, I have been leading a life full of remorse. It's a void home. And a void heart. There is no hope anywhere. I wake up, I do the daily chores, I eat, I sleep. I no longer find a reason to fight for myself. I don't bother myself with any sarcasm or painful stabs of words like before. My parents left for the abode a few years back, due to illness, mostly rooting from the feeling of helplessness for not seeing me in peace ever in life after a wrong marriage. But it was my fate, I never blamed them. They were not strong enough, neither was I. I grew up in a happy middle-class family, with a gentle father and a loving homely mother. We didn't know how to handle a situation of domestic violence 'then'. We suffered- My parents suffered mentally and I suffered in all possible ways. It broke me, my confidence, and my hope to see a better day ever. And my daughter appeared as a tiny tot to keep me alive for so many more years. Now she is gone.

I left the demon the next day after the lifeless body was carried off the premises. I never looked back. But my decision was too late. I found a place to stay at an old-age home and look after the paperwork, to cater to the basic needs. I don't even aspire to do something great. *I was not even strong enough to commit suicide.*

It's a deep-rooted feeling that I failed her as a mother and as a woman. If only I was strong enough to leave the demon when he hit me on the very first day… or at least when he misbehaved with my parents. When he took me to another city only to keep me away from my parent's support, and when he hit my daughter. I hate him for his sick mentality but I also hate myself for living like a 'victim'. Children learn what they see, not what we preach.

My tiny tot saw a weak woman who never stood up for herself… a woman who just kept on living with the bruises, without trying to make things right. Who could not decide her fate… She couldn't stand to see herself in my place. Was she scared of being born as a female? I wonder why I couldn't set a good example for my daughter well within time.

I am remorseful. I hate myself. I don't want to continue breathing any more, as this is what remains in life for me.

I am an ordinary woman. I just wanted a happy home and family to live my life. But you never have an easy life how high or low your aim may be! You have to struggle to make it work for you. I gave up too early in life. Now I am just putting an end to my suffering. My heart has felt heavy past two years. It's time to bid goodbye as my eyes are sleepy. The sleeping pills I had in my dinner might help me meet my daughter in the heavenly abode!

May the women in the world be strong enough to stop being 'VICTIMS' and stand up for themselves! Help begins at home... Take a stand, when things go wrong... and educate your children not just what's in the books BUT to survive in this cruel world... Don't keep them NAIVE... Don't be 'ME'!

It's the night of my freedom, goodnight!

CHAPTER 28

IS SUICIDE ON YOUR MIND?

"SUICIDE is a permanent solution to a TEMPORARY problem."
– Phil Donahue,

An American Media Personality

*J*ust hold on to your breath for a little more, and give it a last thought. After all, it's a big decision and you surely need not hurry. You have been thinking about it lately, and today might be a trigger point... but you surely can live a few more Minutes to reconsider and be sure of it... Because there is no return! And you know this truth, it's escaping forever and not solving anything.

I know a few people in my life who took this step, and I want to share it for any kind of learning you can make out of it, on your own... and then decide.

1. **A teenage girl** - She hung herself with a rope on the ceiling fan. She was the only daughter of her I'll-fated parents, who are still living BROKEN in her memories.

   REASON - Cheated in a love affair.

   After Thought- Her parents have this one thought every day in life, that if only once she had confided in us... the worst scenario would have been a family drama, hurt, tears, and a few days of anger... and it would be OVER in some time.

   Learning- Even if the hurt continues and family drama is not over, have you ever met a person in life who can say that s/he never saw a good thing in life and who never smiled? Who has never seen festivals? Who never met people? Does it sound logical?

   Time never stops! GIVE IT TIME... Problems are TEMPORARY... Emotions keep changing!

2. **A young mother** - She ate sleeping pills and killed herself. She left her child lonely at the hands of fate, and her supporting parents HEARTBROKEN for a lifetime.

   REASON - she lost one of her children a while ago, and she also had an abusive marriage.

   After Thought- Tragedies break us, there is no defying pain and loss of any kind. But life puts you on some responsibilities too... like that of a young child on her mother; of old parents who still live to see a better life for their kids and support them... Your step killed their happiness forever, and the guilt remains in their mind that you were not comfortable reaching out to them... they couldn't help you when you were broken... If the pain of an abusive life and a child's death you felt was unbearable, how could you make your other child and old parents go through the same ordeal? Not fair!

Learning- Find your dot of HOPE! In the darkest of nights, you see the shining star... Find it, live for it... GUILT doesn't help unless you work to make things right for SOMEONE... It might be just ANYONE in NEED!

3. **A husband-** He jumped off the roof of his apartment building. He left her loving wife widowed and toddler fatherless... such a punishment for a lifetime!

REASON- Loss of Job / Financial Crisis / Uncertainties.

After Thought- If once he had reached out to his wife, someone in the family or friends and cried his heart out... asked for help or suggestions... If only he had given himself a chance to start afresh, even something trivial, not of his choice... but it would have saved the future of his family. If not help, INSULT was what he could have faced, but isn't LIFE more valuable than this temporary uncertainty and hardship?

Learning- Be it an insult, anger, frustration, failure, joblessness, cheating, or whatever... It is just a phase and just a human emotion !!! Whether you live or die, the world still goes on... BUT your remorseful death will surely make it more difficult for your LOVED ONES! Do you want that? NO!

4. **A well-settled middle-aged man-** He shot himself in his mouth. Left his old parents mourning for a lifetime. His wife is cursed by society for not understanding him and instigating his death. His kids are unsettled and clueless about why this ordeal when everything looked good. His sibling is unforgivable for not being emotionally available.

REASON- Anger / Hidden Frustration / Alcohol / Heat of a Moment

After Thought- If that one moment of weakness could have been averted !!! If only he had reached out to someone OR someone would have taken the initiative to break the barriers and give him a shoulder to lean on! If only he focused on ONE REASON TO LIVE, rather than many reasons to die...

Learning- In your moment of weakness, REACH OUT to someone or just anyone... even a stranger and find shelter in your emotions! Grab a book or a glass of water or write something, even if it's a suicide note... focus on ONE thing or person or even a memory, which is GOOD in life... And here you are... ALIVE!

Life is too precious to lose it for a temporary emotion or situation. YOU ARE BRAVER THAN YOUR WEAKNESS!!! **Stay strong, stay alive...** You surely will get through this phase sooner or later, just hang on and keep doing your best to stay alive... Isn't this the basic thing of life? Just trying to make it easier to live and live on and on and on !!!

If you find a little worth in my write-up, focus on living your life from the next sunrise you see tomorrow... and till then let go of all thinking and look at the vast sky... **LIFE has many possibilities, suicide ends you in weakness!**

Now, have a glass of water and sleep like a baby! Smile at me...

CHAPTER 29

GRIEF– THE MURDER STORY

PART-1 : The Brutal Murder

It was 10:30 pm of a winter night. The doorbell rang and I saw Ankush's mother walk into our drawing room. She was clad in a bright red cotton nighty and a red shawl over it. It was sometime in the late 80's and we only had landlines and wireless handsets for communication then. She had come to make some important phone call, as her husband had not returned home from bank and his office phone was unanswered last after around 7 pm.

Background: We lived in a flat on the third floor of the apartment building and Ankush lived in the flat on the left side of ground floor. He lived with his mother Preeti and father, fondly called Jain sahib by all flatmates. Jain uncle was a bank employee, a bank manager, posted in a remote area. He used to commute with his scooter, and it was usual to come home late sometimes but never more than 8 pm or so. Ankush was the youngest kid of our group of friends and was about 4-5 years old. Preeti Aunty was a graceful young woman who always looked prim and proper with an effortlessly worn saree, a loosely done bun of her black hair, bright red sindoor and a medium size maroon bindi on her forehead.

Probably 'Red' was her favourite colour as she mostly dressed in different shades of it and looked beautiful. My mother had friendly neighbour relations with Preeti Aunty, and since my father held a respected post of an officer bureaucracy, she hoped to get some help from him for tracing his husband's whereabouts, that night.

The Plot: I was lying in bed with my toddler sister, but all awake and seeing the movement, while waiting for my mother to put us to sleep. As my mother and Preeti aunty sat in the drawing room, my father took the small chit she had about Jain uncle's bank location, and landline phone number etc and came to the bedroom to talk to his network of people who could help at that time. After a few phone calls at the District Magistrates Office and some others, he had sweat on his forehead and some sort of uneasiness in his being.

I saw him push the bedroom door a little so that his voice is not heard outside. He made a few more calls. And I saw tears rolling down his cheeks that he was quick to wipe off. Then he went outside in the drawing room and asked Preeti Aunty to go home and be with Ankush (whom she had put to sleep and came up for help), while he will inform her personally as soon as he gets some information from his sources. Preeti aunty looked better with this assurance and left. She just whispered that she will be waiting to hear about the reason why his husband was getting so very late for the first time ever.

As soon as she left and the door closed after her, my mother got suspicious and asked my father how he couldn't trace it, something he could easily do with his connections. And my father broke the most heartbreaking news ever... "Jain Sahib is NO MORE!" The clock tickled 11 pm. My mother was crying for her dear friend's plight and for the gentleman Jain Sahib, who was a simple respectful man, known only for good reasons. DEATH is a harsh reality. Even more harsh when you find that it was not a natural death.

What my father learnt from the sources was too heartbreaking even to imagine to tell to her wife. He was killed, murdered with bullet wounds, and his body was found in a pool of blood on the roadside pothole by some strangers passing by, who informed the local police. His scooter was found lying on the road about half kilometers away from his body. His colleagues and bank employees were informed but no one mustered the courage to tell it to his family. After all, he lived only with his wife and a small 4-5 year old son, who could break this news? How to do this? And no one came forward.

Same was the plight of my parents, not knowing what to do. They slowly took a few other flatmates in confidence and broke the I'll fated news. The body had been sent for post-mortem and would not have come home before legal formalities, not before early morning. My father took charge to call up his contacts and expedite the process, also contacted the bank colleagues to obtain Jain Sahib's friends and relative contacts near by and parents in other city. My mother went downstairs to Preeti Aunty and mustered all her courage to say that she had come to stay their for the night while my father is trying to trace if there was some road block or accident in that route which is a possibility.

Preeti aunty was suspicious though. That night was one of the longest ever. I remember feeling a little frightened of all this and putting on all the lights of my home, until mumma was back in my room. While my father would occasionally come and see us resting in bed, and was again on call with hospital, police and bank people to bring Jain uncle home, his sweet home! Back to his wife and kid, the last night in his home before he would leave it forever after. There was deafening silence in the building and the surrounding. Dark night, winter, light winds blowing, whispers, murmurs, mourners and silence!

Breaking the News: As we heard it from my mother, it was almost 3 am in the morning that Preeti Aunty asked her straight, "Bhabhi ji, kuch to hua hai... aap bata dijiye mujhe ab!" Yes, she knew in the heart of hearts that something disastrous has happened... may be a terrible accident or some emergency at his parents place or something not so right. My mother burst into tears as she held Preeti Aunty and told her, *"Jain Sahib hum sabko chhor kar chale gaye. Wo ab nahi rahe. Preeti, tumko bahut himmat karni hogi!"* Only the one who has suffered something like this can understand what it would have felt like.

DEATH was black like that night, was more chilling than the winter wind, and there was no return. Preeti aunty was stern. She became a statue. Not a tear dropped from her eloquent eyes. She asked, "Kya hua unhe?" Obviously, murder and illness cannot be a guess for a simple good man who was also young and healthy. The bank colleagues and some neighbors entered the apartment gate with Jain Sahib's lifeless body, clad in white sheet... out from the ambulance at around 5:30 am.

The Murder: Later after investigation, what was talked about is put here. While Jain Sahib was returning from his bank, murderers had followed him to a lonely and blind space on the road. He was targeted and followed for a few day before it. Probably for some favors or bank keys that remained in his custody. It was known that Jain

Sahib was murdered with three bullet wounds.... that too after he was dragged to the roadside pothole and the murderers first tried to kill him by cutting his throat with a sharp knife or something. Even after those cuts on his throat he tried to escape because he had two bullet hits on his back and one on his chest... His body was found about half kilometer away from the scooter... and was probably dragged to the pothole after murder. Death took him. What a pitiful end of a gentleman! What a heartbreaker for the family! What a shock!

PART-2: Life After the Murder

It was just 3 weeks after the gruesome murder of Jain Sahib, Aniket Jain - the bank manager, and life was completely changed for Preeti - his wife and their 4 year old son Ankush. After the funeral, it took just a week for her family to persuade her to pack all the things and leave the posting place immediately either to her parents or Aniket's Parents. That she did, moved to her parents home, in the outskirts of Delhi. After all there was nothing left behind at the place of posting for them if Aniket was no more. No relatives, not many friends, nothing important.

A month just passed by and Preeti put Ankush in a near by school. She was also thinking about her life without Aniket. She loved to be at home and take care of it while Aniket was in bank. She waited for him in the evening and then Ankush went out to play with friends, and the husband wife duo had some refreshing chit-chat discussing their whole day. Later the three of them had dinner together every night, and slept. It was a simple life. Not anymore. Preeti had a long life ahead and she needed to be strong and capable to take care of her son Ankush and... also to her immense joy mixed with surplus sorrow, she tearfully announced to her mother that she was pregnant. Another baby is on its way, fatherless already... What a sarcasm by the supreme power!

Tears rolled down her cheek for several days. Thinking of the life she was supposed to live with Aniket, of this joyous news that she could not tell her dead husband, about all the uncertainties and insecurities she was going through each day. She went to see a doctor for initial check up during pregnancy. The new bloom in her tummy, finally made her move, she had to muster some courage!

She called up Aniket's bank and asked about the ongoing of the investigation. She also seek help to settle his finances and insurance, that they hardly shared as a couple. To a great relief, as per banks policy, soon she got an offer letter from Aniket's bank to work as a clerk, as she was a graduate. She was a little relieved, as things were slowly moving out of darkness. She shifted to a flat on the same floor as her parents and brother's family, and told them that she wanted a separate set up near by as she didn't want to always be dependent. That she had to take care of her pregnancy & kids & also join a new job.

Her family supported her to the utmost. Preeti had decided to move on and let bygones be bygones. Her motherly instinct was above any other feeling of fear or grief. She knew that she had to be a protector and a provider too for her children. Though she never imagined but life was giving her a second inning and she had no choice rather than to take up this challenge. Aniket would never have imagined such a drastic change in Preeti ever in his life.

But if he was around, no doubt, he would have been proud of her courage and determination... Life might be harsh, but it flows like water in a river, it never stops before it reaches its destination! Life goes on and on and on ... and so did Preeti... balanced her pace, kept her memories intact but moved on for the sake of her own mental peace and for the sake of small kids! She chose to shine... Kudos to the strong lady!

The simple graduate housewife took on to be the provider and protector of her home and kids when destiny knocked at her door. She overcame her weakness, her fear and grief... she indeed needs an applause to be so brave!

◆◆◆

CHAPTER 30

MYSTICAL- THE BEAUTIFUL INK BLACK HEART

Grief is a part of everyone's journey. It starts from the time we are born. Every loss prepares us, for the bigger loss, leading to the ultimate one, which is death. Sometimes a soul has a story to tell, even after death.

As death is only of the body, not of the eternal soul. It just changes its body, its course and its pace. Here is the story of someone who had 'the Ink Black Heart', owing it to her capability to see the dead... the souls of the dead!

After a near-death experience when she was about four, Noor woke up to visitors, from the other side. Trauma and spiritual experiences sometimes seem to go hand in hand, and she had just escaped death from one of the tragic road accidents that took away her parents. But it also bestowed her a strange new ability to see those who no longer existed in the real world. She stayed with her mother's younger sister, whom she fondly called 'Nitya Mausi', who meant the world to her. She told her 'Nitya Mausi' in all her innocence that mumma & papa told her that they had to go and that they still loved her.

'Noor' clung to her 'Mausi' saying Mumma wants you to take care of me… And that she and Papa turned into 'a golden ball of light' as they left her in the hospital after the accident. 'Noor' was in a coma for almost three days after the fatal accident, when there was a landslide, and a rock fell over hitting their SUV and damaging it to the core. She was then, sleeping in her mother's lap, and was the only survivor of the mishap. For her unmarried 'Nitya Mausi' who had always loved her unconditionally, it was a new journey of life too. She knew 'Noor' was a chosen one! She had some strange ability, a quiet in her 'big brown eyes'.

In the early instances, it was a few of 'Noor's' friends with whom she played in school and at home, but soon she realized that those little friends of hers were not visible to other eyes. As she grew up, she saw people around, those she knew were her neighbors, teachers, relatives and some strange beings who had 'no shadows'. She heard faint whispers and voices that started getting clearer with age. Though a child, she was quick to learn that she was led into a future, where the gifted can offer closure and support to those in need.

The earlier experiences were a shock for others, especially 'Nitya Mausi' who was shaken to hear from a five-year-old 'Noor' that the 'Dadi Maa' in the neighborhood just come into her bedroom and told her that she had fallen in the washroom, so someone should go and check her there. Nitya Mausi ignored it thinking it to be a child's imagination, but soon found it to be a true incident in a couple of hours. Nitya was scared, and also on alert mode as she started taking 'Noor's' imaginary friends more seriously. 'Noor' would play in her room alone for hours, but Nitya could hear her chatting and giggling as if she was playing with her friends.

Nitya knew now, that she was growing up a special child, and that she needed help from someone more knowledgeable in this field. She did discuss it with a few, but then she didn't want to scare her baby, as 'Noor' seemed to be perfectly normal with her day-to-day scenario. She left it as fate, what was destined for her and would lead her to the purpose of her life. Instead of making her vulnerable to worldly judgments and experiments, she stood in silence to support her.

As she grew up another year or so, she shared with 'Nitya Mausi' about the stranger 'bhaiya' in her bedroom, who requested her to give a message to his mom who lived in the next lane, that he loved her and was sorry for not listening to her. He had died in a 'bike accident' last evening. 'Noor' had started getting woken up by spirits at what could be called 'time of death'. She would get shaken awake and would open her eyes, and there would be someone standing there in front of her. They would say, "I just died. I'm so-and-so's little sister, and I passed away, and this is my name, and this is how I died, and I want you to give them a message because you're going to hear about me."

By now 'Noor' was nearly ten years old, a quiet child, but a bright and nevertheless, a gifted one. She would write down, the message, responsibly in her childish handwriting, and deliver it to 'Nitya Mausi'…who would trust her always and pray to save her girl from any untoward incident. She consoled and stood beside 'Noor' as support, telling her that she had an elusive power that she should use to help the needy, that she was gifted, that she must never be scared… It's shocking to be woken up by something standing there, beside your bed, telling you about the death. But 'Nitya Masi' knew, it was a chosen 'Ink Black Heart' which absorbs the pain and suffering of the ones lost to death… and 'love & innocence' of 'Noor' was the supreme power that kept her strong, unscarred, intriguing but accepting the unusual happenings of her life.

It has been years, but even today, sometimes 'Noor' still gets scared of waking up to a stranger beside the bed, then adjusts to it. She would first see the human form very clearly when they just die, and come to meet her. Imagine when you see someone with your eyes open in the dark, and then later after your eyes have adjusted a bit… She could see an outline, and see their eyes, but couldn't see everything. But once they give their message to 'Noor', when they leave, they turn into a ball of beautiful light that flickers in different colors. It's beautiful.

Sometimes, it doesn't necessarily have to make sense to 'Noor' about what message she has been given, but she just has to give what she gets. It's like delivering the envelope and not opening it, not at all trying to decide what the message means. Anything we have touched will retain some energy. So, she does believe that since she touched the realms of the other world in her near-death experience, she got this strange power of absorbing so much of other's pain in her 'Ink Black Heart'! She knows that everything is working for our greater good.

Life is not meant to be easy— if it was, our souls would not evolve. She is just the *'chosen medium'* for the dead, to reach their loved ones one last time, and her beautiful black heart is the cushion for her greater endeavors in exploring the purpose of life!!!

EPILOGUE

Yes I looked back… To see how far I have come, when I chose to MOVE ON!

– `SOULTINKER'

ACKNOWLEDGEMENT

𝒯hank you *@InspiringJatin* without whose guidance this book wouldn't have been possible, that too in record time of less than a week! You brought up an occasion to motivate me to work on this book and complete it with all my dedication to get it published so soon.

Thanks to my family and friends for supporting me in all possible ways and showing your faith in me always!

ABOUT THE AUTHOR

Swapnil Roy 'SOULTINKER'

I am a frank, cheerful, ambitious, adventurous and possessive woman, very much in love with life. I play all those natural roles of being a daughter, a sister, a wife, a DIL, SIL etc. but I am mostly occupied with my role of a mother of two kids- a boy and a girl, both equally naughty and cute at the same time.

To the best of my intentions, I am sincere in relationships and responsibilities, and things that matter to me... and I value friendship a lot. I love reading, writing, travelling and gardening... all this while listening to or murmuring a song!

If I have missed telling something you wish to know about me, you may safely consider guessing what a 'Typical Aries Woman' is all about... It will probably be true for me, leaving exceptions.

Academically, I have earned a degree as a Bachelor of Engineering in Mechanical Branch. Later did a Post Graduate Diploma in Business Administration with a specialization in Human Resource Management. Working as an HR is my forte and I love my work. My First Book 'Human or Humor Resource' would give you a glimpse of my outlook towards my work.

With a few jobs on and off, even while studying, I have some experience with multinationals, private as well as govt sector, and I continue to enjoy my time working and learning just anywhere, be it home or office. (Height of Flexibility with a Pinch of Rigidity that makes me so moody!)

Nevertheless, as you read my books, blogs, write-ups, comments etc. you will surely get to know me better and form your own opinion about me... So, till then, I hope the above information will satisfy your curiosity about me as an AUTHOR! *Happy Reading...*

BOOKS BY THE AUTHOR

Book1: *<u>Human or Humor Resource: HR Tales That Will Make You Chuckle & Rethink the 9-to-5 Stories</u>*

This book has handy information for the freshers' who are taking up their first job as a professional in life, and it also is a refresher for anyone who is feeling anxious about joining a new job and leaving the old company and things behind.

In this book you will find the psychology of an employee all through his/her work life, the feelings at the time of joining or while in office, thoughts when getting a promotion or while retiring. Everyone goes through these phases of work life.

The fear, joy, anxiety, hopes, disappointments, rules, etiquettes etc. are all covered in simple words, easy to understand and practice too on an immediate basis.

This book comes to you as an easy and simple walkthrough to help you with your day-to-day office life.

You may want to delve into it whenever you feel and get some encouragement by brushing up the basic skills and positive attitude suitable for any job for that matter. It's best advised to keep it as a handy companion.

Funny incidents, HR Jokes, Motivational Quotes, and Inspiring ideas are available throughout the book.

Book2: _Maverick at Forty Something Be One Hell of a Woman!_

A Non-Fiction Self Help Book By Swapnil Roy 'SOULTINKER'

In her 'Forties', getting the kids and household a little manageable by now, women may redefine their roles, passions, and priorities. It's time to get up, dress up and show up. It's time to explore. Whether it's pursuing a new hobby, career change, or travel, midlife is an opportunity for reinvention.

This book discusses how and why should you intentionally emphasize on self-acceptance. Women often face societal pressures related to appearance, career, and family. Now in your 'Forties' it's high time to empower yourself and embrace your uniqueness and value.

One should live like a 'Maverick' - *"Independent in behavior or thought, kind of unconventional or rebel"*.

Midlife empowerment is a topic that resonates with many women as they navigate the complexities of this life stage. This book reiterates from beginning to end as how women may find purpose in their life, beyond societal norms. They just have to be courageous to make their way and take small steps each and every day towards their dream life. Midlife may be the most conducive time to build supportive networks, friendships, mentorships, and community involvement. It will provide emotional sustenance, and then midlife can most likely be liberating to the hilt. This book is all about it !

A MUST READ FOR EVERY WOMAN !!!

www.ingramcontent.com/pod-product-compliance
Lightning Source LLC
LaVergne TN
LVHW041710070526
838199LV00045B/1282